Britannia Sickens

Sir Arthur Wellesley and

'Britannia sickens, Cintra!
at thy name'
BYRON

Britannia Sickens

the Convention of Cintra

by

MICHAEL GLOVER

LEO COOPER : LONDON

First published in 1970 by
LEO COOPER LIMITED
196 Shaftesbury Avenue
London wc1

ISBN 0 85052 047 9

Printed in Great Britain by
Clarke, Doble and Brendon Limited
at Plymouth

CONTENTS

MAPS

Drawn by Boris Weltman

ACKNOWLEDGEMENTS

The author and publishers are grateful to the following for permission to reproduce copyright illustrations: The Mansell Collection Nos. 1, 4, 6, 7 and 8; E. M. Knight Esq., No. 2; The National Gallery of Scotland, No. 3; The National Portrait Gallery, No. 5.

ILLUSTRATIONS

Introduction

IT was a hundred years and a day between Marlborough's victory at Oudenarde and the day on which Sir Arthur Wellesley first sailed for the Peninsula. Between those two dates the British army sank from a position in which it was recognised as being, for its numbers, the most effective force in Europe to one in which its allies and its enemies alike regarded it with something approaching contempt. Its defeat in the American War of Independence was its most spectacular failure but in the early years of the French Revolutionary war it reached depths of incompetence and ineffectiveness which far surpassed its showing in America. A talented young staff officer, who spent seven years as Under Secretary of State for War, wrote of those days: 'Men of the present generation can hardly form an idea of what the military forces of England really were when the great war broke out in 1793. Our army was lax in its discipline, entirely without system, and very weak in its numbers. Each colonel of a regiment managed it according to his own notions, or neglected it altogether. There was no uniformity of drill or movement; professional pride was rare; professional knowledge still more so. Never was a kingdom less prepared for a stern and arduous conflict.' Force is added to this description by the fact that it was written at a time when Britain was at another low point in her military history – just before the outbreak of the Crimean war.

This ill-success had been achieved despite the availability of magnificent raw material. The potentiality of the British soldier is as great as any in the world. The superb tradition of the British infantryman runs steadily from Hastings through Agincourt, the Dunes, Blenheim, Minden, Waterloo and Inkerman to Mons and beyond. Nor was there a shortage of competent commanders, Ligonier and Wolfe would have been ornaments to any army. The root of the trouble lay in the system, if it can be so described, which controlled all British military operations. The ramifications of this system were so complex and the multifarious authorities of which it was composed so ill coordinated that it might be thought that it had been designed to thwart any military operation that might be proposed. It was backed by a press and a public opinion that, while expecting the army to achieve feats well beyond its strength, grudged every penny that was spent on it. By 1808 the British had become so inured to military failure that they scarcely hoped for anything else. It was of the obstacles raised by his own countrymen that Sir Ralph Abercromby spoke when he remarked that 'There are risks in a British warfare, unknown in any other service.'

Arthur Wellesley, Duke of Wellington, was the first British general since Marlborough who had sufficient ability not only to defeat the enemy but to be able to surmount the difficulties set in his path by his colleagues, his political masters and the mass of his fellow countrymen. While it is true that, in doing so, he was greatly helped by the military reforms initiated by the Duke of York, Lord Castlereagh, Sir David Dundas and Sir John Moore, it cannot be denied that the victories in the Peninsula and at Waterloo were Wellington's personal triumphs. Other commanders had the advantage of these reforms but, while Wellington was winning victories in Spain and Portugal, British troops, with numerical advantage, were being defeated at Walcheren, Tarragona and Bergen-op-Zoom.

The history of the Portuguese campaign of 1808 is less

important for its purely military aspects, for telling how Welles-ley defeated Junot and his army, than because it is the story of how Wellesley won his first, and crucial, round with the British tradition for waging war, compounded as it was of inefficiency, ossified tradition, divided responsibility and a public clamour compounded equally of ignorance and malice.

1

'Two Spanish Noblemen

JUNE 1808. There was little for the newspapers to publish. 'The late warmth in the weather has in some degree abolished the sarsnet pelisse adopted in the early part of the season; and mantles, French cloaks, Grecian scarves and pelisses of fine white muslin are substituted in their place.' At Leominster a sow-pig was tapped for the dropsy and 'full sixteen gallons of water were taken from her.' She recovered. In the Manchester area the weavers were rioting. Some who were arrested and put in the New Prison at Rochdale were rescued by the mob and the prison burned to the ground. Consequently a report from Nottingham told how on 3rd June 'at eight o'clock a *dispatch route* was received by the 2nd battalion of the 45th Foot to march *forthwith* to Manchester. Many of the officers were enjoying the innocent delights of the theatre, when the abrupt appearance of the Sergeant-Major in the boxes broke the illusion, by announcing the intelligence that they were summoned to parade. The men were widely spread through this large town, many of them regaling with Nottingham ale. However, much to the honour of the regiment, and highly creditable to its discipline, the whole were under arms and in marching order in less than two hours from the time the route was received.'

The 4th of June was the king's birthday. 'His Majesty completed his seventieth year, and although arrived at this advanced age, enjoys the most excellent health and spirits, and great vigour of mind and body. The Bishops of Chester and Salisbury, several dignified clergymen, and a select party of personages of distinction were admitted to His Majesty's presence, to pay their respects, the disorder in his eyes still preventing him from appearing in public.' In the afternoon the Queen held a drawing room and 'persons of all descriptions from the country flocked to view the numerous assemblage of nobility, persons of distinction, and gentry going to court in their costly and superb dresses; and although they certainly may be called antiquated, yet it is rather a novel sight to behold them, since Her Majesty holds so few courts. The streets were crowded to an excess. . . . The Duchess of Bedford went to Court in a very superior style of grandeur to any other visitor. She went in a chair preceded by three footmen in new state liveries, far surpassing any we ever saw.'[1] Queen Charlotte, wearing a blond lace petticoat, beautifully ornamented with rich diamond bands, two large diamond bows at the pocket holes, 'received her guests with her usual affability and condescension.' They included, apart from

13

five non-royal dukes and six marquesses, Lieutenant-General Sir Arthur Wellesley, Chief Secretary for Ireland, and Lieutenant-General Sir Harry Burrard, Governor of Calshott Castle. The latter had, that morning, attended H.R.H. the Duke of York, the Commander in Chief, when the colour of the Third Guards was trooped on Horse Guards Parade.

That evening the Royal Dukes dined with their parents; the Foreign Secretary, Mr. Canning, gave a dinner for the diplomatic corps; the Home Secretary for the Lord Mayor and Sheriffs of London, and the Prime Minister for such members of the Cabinet as were not dining with either the Home or the Foreign Secretaries. On a less formal level there was a good deal of merry-making in the streets and 'a number of idle men and boys assembled in Catherine Street in The Strand and let off squibs and fire-works in the most mischievous manner. The windows of the houses were broken by brickbats and stones, particularly the house of Mr. Johnstone, the machinist of Drury Lane theatre. His door was knocked at, and when the door was opened by the sister of Mrs. Johnstone, a fellow thrust a blazing squib at her, which set fire to her clothes. Her screams brought the assistance of the whole family, and by great exertions they extinguished the flames, but not until her pelisse was nearly destroyed and her back and shoulders very much burned. Mr. Johnstone went into the street to endeavour to discover and secure the incendiary, but in making the attempt he had his pocket picked of bank notes to the value of £10.'[2]

To crown a memorable day the Poet Laureate, Henry James Pye, composed a birthday ode:

Not with more joy, when, gathering round
Dark mists the face of heaven deform,
When howls the wind with hollow sound,
Preluding to the rising storm;
We thro' the severing clouds descry
Of cheering light a golden beam;
That now, when spreading wide and far,
Roars the tremendous peal of war,

14

We bless the peace and joy the ray,
That gilds the happy hours of George's Natal Day.

Had the poet not allowed himself a generous measure of
artistic licence he would have had to admit that 'the tremendous
peal of war', far from roaring was, in Britain, distinctly muted.
For more than fifteen years, with only one short interval, Britain
had been at war with France, yet not since the summer of 1806
had a British soldier discharged his musket within range of a
Frenchman. The Royal Navy kept up its ceaseless blockade
around the coasts of Napoleon's Empire and constantly harried
the few French ships which ventured on the high seas, but the
French army had not been engaged by British troops since the
egocentric Sir John Stuart had made his victorious, if pointless,
foray to Maida. Faced with a French Empire which comprised,
besides France, the whole of Italy, the Netherlands and most of
Germany; at war with Denmark, Spain, Prussia and Russia, with
Austria and Turkey as hostile neutrals and Portugal in French
occupation, the British government was at a loss to know how
to proceed. It was not an inspiring government. The Prime Minister, the Duke of Portland, was 'both dull and ill'[3] and the only
two senior ministers of real talent, Castlereagh, the Secretary
for War and the Colonies, and Canning, the Foreign Secretary,
cordially detested each other. Recent British warlike acts, not
all of which could be blamed on the Portland ministry, included
a peculiarly abortive naval demonstration off Constantinople, an
invasion followed by a humiliating evacuation of Egypt, and a
disastrous attempt to seize Buenos Aires, which resulted in the
surrender of the whole force engaged. The general commanding
at Buenos Aires, John Whitelocke, who had behaved throughout
with striking ineptitude, was, on his return, court-martialled and
sentenced to be 'cashiered and declared totally unfit and un-
worthy to serve His Majesty in any capacity whatever.' It was
a just sentence but it inevitably called into question the abilities
of the ministers who had given him the command. In fact, the
government stayed in power less through its abilities than because
there was no acceptable alternative in sight. The Whig Opposition

15

was disunited and factious. Its more radical members were widely believed, and not without justice, to favour making concessions to Napoleon. Its moderate wing had filled the principal positions in the short-lived 'Ministry of All the Talents' of 1806–7 and had shown themselves even more incapable of managing the war than the Duke of Portland and the Tories.

If, in 1808, the British prosecution of the war was in the doldrums, that of France was at its peak. Napoleon Bonaparte was Emperor of the French, King of Italy, Mediator of the Swiss Republic and Protector of the Confederation of the Rhine. One of his brothers was King of Holland, another of Naples, a third of Westphalia. The King of Spain was his faithful ally. Dalmatia and the Hanseatic towns were his satrapies. Between 1805 and 1807, in an astonishing series of victories – Ulm, Austerlitz, Jena and Friedland – he had shattered the military power of Austria, Prussia and Russia. He had dictated peace in Vienna and Berlin. In July 1807 he had, at Tilsit, concluded with the Czar of all the Russias a treaty whereby they partitioned Europe between them and concerted measures to defeat Britain.

Ineffective as was Britain's military effort, Napoleon knew that his Empire could never be secure until he had destroyed her power. He led an incomparable army but it could not serve him against Britain unless he could secure the means to transport it across the Straits of Dover. To do this he must overmatch the Royal Navy which, since his last attempt to do so had foundered off Cape Trafalgar, enjoyed a supremacy which was all but absolute. While this was being achieved he set about destroying Britain's overseas trade by closing every port under his control to British goods. At Tilsit the Czar undertook to do the same. Between them, the two Emperors controlled every European port, outside the Turkish Empire, except those of Denmark, Portugal and Sweden. Once she had been driven from Pomerania, the problem of Sweden was left to Russia, which proceeded to filch Finland. The subjugation of Denmark and Portugal came into the French sphere of operations.

The French moves against both had two aims – to close their

16

ports and to seize their navies. With these in his hands Napoleon believed that he would have the strength to land the *Grande Armée* in Kent. As things stood the fleets available to him consisted of seventy-five French and Dutch ships of the line, in varying states of repair, twenty-four from Spain and thirty from Russia, in all 129 battleships. Against these the Royal Navy had a strength which fluctuated between 103 and 113 ships of the line. Already France and her allies had a clear numerical superiority but the French took the realistic view that, since the Royal Navy had kept to the seas for years while the French and Spanish ships had been blockaded in their ports, the British would have a great qualitative advantage. A French naval appreciation very justly declared 'we shall be able to make peace with safety when we have 150 ships of the line.' The Danish fleet had seventeen battleships, the Portuguese ten. Joined to the allied fleets, these would bring the strength up to 156. All that remained was to secure them.

To the astonishment of the Emperor, he was forestalled. The British intelligence did a remarkable job at Tilsit. On 7th July 1807 the Treaty by which the French seizure of Denmark was agreed was signed on a raft on the eastern borders of Prussia, under conditions of the greatest secrecy. So fast did the news reach London that by the 19th of the same month naval and military commanders had received their orders for an expedition to Copenhagen. On 3rd August twenty-seven British battleships and 26,000 troops arrived off that city and demanded the surrender of the Danish fleet. Not unnaturally the Danes, hitherto neutral, refused and prepared to resist. It was not until Copenhagen had been besieged, bombarded and, in substantial sections, burned to the ground that they agreed to hand over their ships, which were promptly sailed back to 'safe-keeping' in British ports. It was a high-handed act and the Opposition did not hesitate to brand it as piracy. Napoleon, simultaneously, made a striking display of outraged self-righteousness, occupied Denmark with French troops and pressed on with his plans to occupy neutral Portugal.

A French army occupied Lisbon without opposition on 30th

November 1807, supported by three Spanish divisions. The British made no attempt to land troops to support their old ally, but as French troops approached the capital the Portuguese fleet, carrying the Prince Regent and his family, sailed out of the Tagus estuary for Brazil under the escort of a squadron of the Royal Navy commanded by Rear-Admiral Sir Sidney Smith, who had earlier played a notable part in thwarting Napoleon's plans by his defence of Acre.

Disappointed as he was by his failure to secure the Portuguese fleet, Napoleon still had the satisfaction of closing the ports of Lisbon and Oporto to British, indeed, to all, trade. Moreover, there was an ulterior purpose to his occupation of Portugal. He had determined to bring Spain under his direct control. As early as 1805, in conversation with Marshal Jourdan, 'he repeated several times that a Bourbon on the throne of Spain was too dangerous a neighbour.'[4] In November 1807, while French and Spanish troops were marching in alliance on Lisbon, the Emperor offered the Spanish crown to his brother Joseph, King of Naples. To this end, and ostensibly to support his 'Army of Portugal', the Emperor marched more than 90,000 troops into Spain between December 1807 and March 1808. Far from marching to the support of their colleagues in Portugal, these large reinforcements quartered themselves comfortably between the French frontier and Burgos, except for one substantial corps which settled itself around Barcelona, a city not, by the wildest flights of fancy, on the road to Portugal.

Napoleon had claimed that the Spanish Bourbons were dangerous neighbours. It is hard to believe that King Charles IV could be a danger to any one. He was weak-willed almost to the point of feeble-mindedness and wholly under the influence of his vicious, ineffective queen, Maria Luisa who, in turn was dependent on her lover, the chief minister and Captain-General, Manuel Godoy, the Prince of the Peace. Godoy, a vain and avaricious patron of the arts, had been bribed by Napoleon by the promise of a sovereign principality hacked out of southern Portugal. This to him was a vital piece of life insurance since he was on the worst possible terms with the heir apparent,

18

Ferdinand, Prince of the Asturias. Bitterly as the Spanish people resented the creeping French occupation of their country, the King, the Queen and Godoy did nothing to avert it and Godoy, who was popularly believed to have invited the French troops into Spain, sank to a level of unpopularity unknown even to him. As Godoy's stock sank, that of Prince Ferdinand rose, despite the fact that his only virtue was his detestation of Godoy, being otherwise as weak and worthless as his father.

In mid-March the French troops, headed by Marshal Murat, Grand Duke of Berg and brother-in-law to the Emperor, started marching from Burgos to Madrid, giving out that they were bound for Gibraltar. The Royal family was at its summer palace at Aranjuez, twenty-five miles south of Madrid, when the news of the French advance reached them. Godoy decided, not before time, that some definite step should be taken and gave orders for the court, escorted by the Madrid garrison, to set out for Seville. Once in Andalusia it would be easy, if the worst came to the worst, to follow the example of the Portuguese Royal Family and take ship for South America. The mob, however, had had more than enough of Manuel Godoy and when the news of the court's impending flight became known, he was set upon and barely escaped with his life. Three days of riot followed at the end of which King Charles, to protect the Favourite's life, abdicated in favour of his son. King Ferdinand, however, soon showed his inadequacy. His first act was to go to Madrid, welcome Murat on his entry into the city and throw himself upon the mercy of Napoleon.

The former king, having, at Murat's instigation, withdrawn his abdication, also implored Napoleon's protection. Thus, the Emperor was in the position of arbitrator and did not hesitate to exploit his advantage. By the end of April, King Ferdinand, King Charles, Queen Maria Luisa and Godoy were all collected at Bayonne where they were confronted by Napoleon in person. A few days of intermixed cajolery and threats sufficed to induce both kings to renounce their rights to the throne and to petition Napoleon to give Spain a king from his own family. He was happy to oblige.

19

Little of this was known in Madrid. With French troops occupying the capital and all the country between it and the French frontier, Napoleon was able to impose an almost complete censorship on news from Bayonne. Some reports and rumours did, however, reach the Junta of Regency in Madrid and leaked out to the populace. Tension built up steadily until Murat gave orders for the remaining members of the Royal Family to be taken to France. That was the flash point. On 2nd May, the *Dos de Mayo* immortalised by Goya, the Madrid mob rose spontaneously against the invaders. The riot, though costing several hundred lives, was easily put down by the French soldiers since, with the gallant exception of some gunners, the Spanish troops did nothing in support of their countrymen. Murat believed that he had settled the whole business. As late as 18th May he wrote to his master that 'the country is tranquil, the state of public opinion in the capital far happier than could have been hoped, and the native soldiery showing an excellent disposition.' He was, however, misinformed. As soon as the news of *Dos de Mayo* spread through Spain, every province burst into revolt against the French. The Asturias led the way.

* * *

Both Murat and Napoleon attributed the outbreak in Madrid to British agents. In fact, the British were not only innocent but, regrettably, ignorant. Their disposable force was, at the best of times, not large and the largest part of it, 11,000 men under Sir John Moore, were, in June 1808, lying packed into troop transports in the harbour of Gothenburg while their commander tried to concert some operation against the French with the King of Sweden. King Gustav, who was mad, was interested only in fighting the Russians in Finland and relations between Britain and her only ally sank to such a low level that, on King Gustav's orders, Moore was placed under house arrest in Stockholm.

The rest of the 'Disposable Force' was in two divisions. One, consisting of about 8,000 infantry, was at Cork; the other, 4,000 infantry under Major-General Brent Spencer,* lay at Gibraltar. In all these immediately available forces there was only one regiment of cavalry, some German Hussars with Moore. At a lesser state of readiness were two brigades of infantry, about 4,000 men, who were preparing for overseas service at east coast ports. Beyond them, a few battalions could be pared off the home garrison and, if a sufficiently tempting opportunity could be seen, there was always the ultimate sign that Britain meant business, the embarkation of a brigade of the Household Troops. Cavalry was in plentiful supply, there being more than thirty regiments on the home strength, but the government was most unwilling to part with any of them, in view of the prevailing industrial unrest and the high cost of fitting out horse transports.

The government, since its brisk and efficient intervention in Denmark, was deficient in military plans save for a somewhat nebulous plan to use the troops at Cork and those at Gibraltar augmented by battalions from the West Indies and Canada to capture the Spanish colonies between Mexico and the Orinoco. The command of this enterprise had been tentatively assigned to a member of the government, Lieutenant-General Sir Arthur Wellesley, Chief Secretary for Ireland. Sir Arthur was, with his usual application, making all the necessary arrangements but he let it be known that he was not greatly enamoured of the scheme. Towards the end of May he came forward with the suggestion that the proper target for the troops immediately available was Spain since the situation there would appear to be 'a crisis in which a great effort might be made with advantage. . . . If it should be found impractical to make any impression upon the French Authority in Spain' the South American plan could be resumed.[5]

Wellesley was not alone in thinking that a fruitful field for the British army could be found in Spain. What was lacking was any definite news about what was happening in Spain. The

* Brent Spencer (1760–1828). Later second in command to Wellington in Portugal (1810–11). A loyal but not over intelligent general who always referred to the Tagus as the Thames.

21

Intelligence Service, which had performed so brilliantly at Tilsit, had not a single agent in the Peninsula, and information coming out of Spain was confined to what could be gleaned from the officially controlled French press and an occasional garbled story from an adventurous sea captain. It was known that large French forces had entered Spain peacefully, that King Charles and the heir apparent had gone to Bayonne and that there had been a great anti-French riot in Madrid. It was believed, and certainly hoped, that there was widespread disaffection against the invaders but, as late as 7th June, the *Morning Chronicle* wrote in its leading article that 'It does not appear that any party or person of consequence has yet ventured to erect a standard of resistance to Bonaparte.'

Only in the south of Spain had the British government a not unsatisfactory channel of communication with the Spanish authorities. The commander of the garrison of Gibraltar, Lieutenant-General Sir Hew Dalrymple, had since his appointment in 1806 been in 'direct and confidential communication' with General Xavier Castaños, commanding the Spanish troops who were besieging Gibraltar. This communication was, in Sir Hew's words, 'productive of mutual convenience, and, to the garrison, it produced an ample supply of many useful articles of provision, and, at the same time, afforded to the British merchants the means of carrying on their commercial speculations with facility and advantage.'[6] At the time of the Franco-Spanish invasion of Portugal, Castaños broke off the exchange, but it was soon afterwards renewed through an accredited but confidential agent, 'a native merchant of Gibraltar named Viali. . . . The communications from Algeciras to this gentleman were frequently by letter, under feigned names and figurative expressions; but on more important occasions, by meetings in the Spanish lines, between Mr. Viali and the secretary of General Castaños.'[7]

By April 1808 Sir Hew, an intelligent, if cautious, man, had been convinced that Spain was ready to rise against the French occupation. On 8th April he reported that the Spanish 'nation was preparing to support its monarch; that Catalonia, Aragon

22

and Valencia had already offered to raise and maintain an army of 150,000 men; and that it was not doubted that the example would be universally followed.' In the circumstances Sir Hew was anxious for instructions. He told Castaños that if the King of Spain should wish to seek asylum from the French in Gibraltar, he would be glad to receive him but that, 'under the present circumstances, which were not, and could not have been, foreseen by His Majesty's government, I had no authority to treat, and could therefore stipulate little or nothing, except by reference to the King, my master.' Very properly, therefore, he wrote on 8th April, asking to be 'honoured by His Majesty's commands'. He received no answer and had written five subsequent dispatches before Castlereagh sent a reply on 25th May.*

Left to his own devices, Sir Hew attempted to secure what seemed to him to be the main essentials for British policy – that neither the Spanish fleet nor the Spanish colonies should fall into French hands and that the French squadron at Cadiz, five sail of the line and a frigate surviving from Trafalgar, should be secured. In this he was perfectly correct. He further, however, endeavoured to secure a Spanish port, either Ceuta or Cadiz, as a base for British troops. Such a proposition would have had the fullest support of the government in London but the Spaniards resolutely refused to discuss it, affecting to believe that the British were attempting to secure a second Gibraltar.

Lack of orders from London was not Sir Hew's only trouble. The French seizure of Madrid had driven the Spaniards back to their old provincial loyalties. Each province determined to fight its own war and jealously guarded any regular troops that happened to be within its borders. Another result of this intense regionalism was that information tended not to get passed from one province to another and such information as reached the far south of the kingdom was frequently in a garbled form. Thus, the first accounts of the meeting at Bayonne, reported that it had been agreed that 'Prince Ferdinand should be acknowledged

* Letters between Gibraltar and London took between two and three weeks. Dalrymple's letter of 8th April reached London not later than 27th April.

23

King of Spain and the Indies and that he should have the administration of Portugal until a general peace; but that Spain should accede to the Confederation of the Rhine, furnishing a contingent of 50,000 men, and should give France a free port in South America.'[8] The dream of dominion over Portugal was one which no Spaniard could resist and all Castaños' plans for resisting the French were momentarily suspended until news filtered through of the *Dos de Mayo* and the forced abdication of both kings.

Even this clear indication of the French treachery did nothing to co-ordinate the Spanish resistance. Independent Juntas sprang up in every province. The Junta established at Seville arrogated to itself the title of Supreme Junta of Spain and the Indies but the other Juntas would not acknowledge its pretensions. Even in its subsidiary role as Supreme Junta for the Four Kingdoms of Andalusia, Seville could not secure the use of the troops from the Andalusian kingdom of Granada without a formal treaty of alliance in which the Granadans insisted on inserting the words 'Seville does not support its independence for its own particular interest.' All these manœuvres and uncertainties would have taxed the ingenuity of a more skilled diplomat than Dalrymple and his dispatches, through no fault of his own, did nothing to clear the mind of the ministry in London. His only positive achievement was to persuade the merchants of Gibraltar to raise an interest free loan of 40,000 dollars to enable Castaños' army to take the field.

He introduced into the discussions in London one complicating factor. When proposing that British troops should garrison Ceuta, on what must have seemed to the Spaniards the highly specious grounds that the whole of the Spanish garrison would be needed in the field, he was faced with the counter-proposal that the Spaniards 'would require from us at least 8 or 10,000 men (besides money); and asked whether, independent of that number, we had more to spare for Ceuta.' Sir Hew returned no answer to this proposal since firstly, he had not that number of troops at his command, and secondly because he suspected that 'the observation, probably made at the moment by the

General's Secretary [was intended] to parry the proposition about Ceuta.'[9] He duly reported, however, to London, where it caused consternation and confusion.

Castlereagh's letter of 25th May, the answer to Sir Hew's request, dated 8th April, for instructions, reached Gibraltar on 8th June. Sir Hew was astonished to find that London had assumed that he had committed himself to assisting Castaños with 10,000 men and to be told that 'the utmost exertion will be made to send out a reinforcement from hence, so as to enable His Majesty to afford the loyal party in Spain the assistance of 10,000 men, which General Castaños seems to require, including what can be spared from the garrison of Gibraltar.' The value of this assurance was, however, largely nullified by the proviso that, 'the most useful manner in which such a corps could be employed seems to be the occupation of some garrison or post near the sea, which it is essential to occupy, and which would liberate an equal or a greater proportion of Spanish troops; and in this view, you will particularly direct your attention to Cadiz.' Dalrymple already knew this proposal to be unacceptable to the Spaniards. For some weeks past General Spencer's small force had been cruising off Cadiz waiting for an opportunity to land. They continued to do so for several weeks to come but no permission was forthcoming. It was not until 1810 that the Spaniards allowed British troops into Cadiz.

Nor did the remainder of Castlereagh's instructions give Dalrymple much comfort or useful guidance. 'His Majesty's approbation' for his actions so far was conveyed to him but His Majesty's ministers were too ill-informed to make constructive suggestions. 'In case the Royal Dynasty should be removed, measures will be taken to secure Spanish America. You will of course look to this contingency with the utmost anxiety, as it must be of the utmost importance that the resources of those opulent provinces should not fall into the hands of the French.' This was clearly wise, but hardly a proposal to put before the Spaniards who were already suspicious of British motives. For the rest, 'His Majesty entertains a full reliance upon your vigour and discretion, in the present juncture: that as, on the one hand, you will not commit either the faith of his government, or the force under your command unnecessarily, or for an inadequate object, you will, on the other, act with determination and spirit, according to circumstances on the spot, relying upon the disposition of His Majesty's government to give your exertions the fullest support.'[10] Sir Hew did not have to be a genius to interpret these instructions as meaning that the government had little or no idea what to do, that he should do what he thought best and they would support him if he did the right thing.

*   *   *

On 8th June, the day on which Sir Hew received Lord Castlereagh's letter, England suddenly became acutely conscious of the war in the Peninsula. The *Sun*, an evening paper supporting the government, wrote: 'This morning about seven o'clock, two Spanish noblemen, viz. Viscount Materosa, and Don Diego de la Vega, arrived at the Admiralty accompanied by Captain Hill of the *Humber*. These noblemen landed at Falmouth from the *Stag*, privateer, to which vessel they had made their way in an open boat from Gijon, a sea port in the province of Asturias, and offered the captain five hundred guineas to convey them to England. The intelligence they bring is of the utmost importance respecting the disposition which prevails to resist the treacherous invasion of the French. It appears that, in consequence of the outrageous and barefaced conduct of the French tyrant, the whole province of Asturias had risen in arms, and 40,000 men had been embodied into an army. They had abundance of arms but ammunition was rather scarce. The same spirit prevailed in Galicia, where the population were rising *en masse*, and commissioners had been sent there to organise a regular military force. So general was the detestation of the French in these provinces that even the women were desirous of taking up arms in defence of their country. The inhabitants of St. Andero [Santander] had manifested their determination not to submit to the French usurpation, in the most decisive manner, and had actually issued a formal declaration of war

26

against the French. It was very generally supposed that the inhabitants of Catalonia and Biscay would follow the noble example which had been set them by Asturias and Galicia; indeed there appeared to be but one sentiment in the minds of the people of Spain with respect to the treacherous and atrocious conduct of the French.'

The Delegates brought with them a letter from the General Assembly of Representatives of the Asturias addressed to 'The Magnanimous Monarch of Great Britain' announcing that the province had openly taken 'arms in their defence to recover the Monarchy, although they cannot recover the persons of their sovereigns. . . . The Principality, therefore, through its Deputies furnished with full powers, presents itself to solicit from your Majesty the succours necessary in their present situation . . . and they hope that your Majesty will deign to attend to their earnest solicitations.

'May the Lord preserve the important life of your Majesty.'[11]

The Press was quick to take up the Spanish cause. The *Courier* asserted that 'There cannot be a doubt that a most favourable opportunity has occurred for this country to do something'. The *Morning Chronicle* said that, assuming the facts were true, 'we are not without hopes that the sentiments with which a portion, and we flatter ourselves, no inconsiderable portion, of the Spanish nation seems to be animated, may lead to very important results. . . . In as far as this country is concerned, we trust that neither lukewarmness nor selfishness will be allowed to influence the conduct of the government on this occasion. Spain is no longer our enemy when she ceases to act under the control of France. By assisting Spain against France we should be fighting our own battles; we should be opposing a mound to the over-whelming tide of conquest before it reaches our shores. . . . We must, however, earnestly deprecate Ministers taking any of their own acts as models. Of plundering and marauding expeditions we have had quite enough; and the Spaniards in the old world will be but little disposed to thank us for that sympathy which would manifest itself by seizing upon their possessions in the new.'[12]

27

Viscount Materosa was accredited as Ambassador from the Spanish Patriots and accommodated in a large house in Hanover Square. His secretary, Don Diego, was sent back to the Asturias, with a letter from Mr. Canning assuring the Junta that 'His Majesty is disposed to afford every assistance and support to an effort so magnanimous and praiseworthy. In pursuance of this disposition, His Majesty has directed such articles of military supply as have been described as most immediately necessary, to be shipped without delay for the port of Grijon, and has ordered a British naval force to be detached to the coast of Asturias, sufficient to protect them against any attempt which might be made by France to introduce troops by sea into that country. Every ulterior effort will be cheerfully made by His Majesty in support of so just a cause.'[13]

By 10th June the papers were full of reports that 'our ministers have determined to aid the cause of the Patriots in Spain. Sir Arthur Wellesley sets off this day or tomorrow for the purpose of proceeding to Spain. He is to take such troops as are in readiness with him, and the force collected at Cork is to follow him.'[14] Possibly aware that this report of Sir Arthur's departure was somewhat at variance with reports on another page of the same paper of Wellesley peacefully guiding the Dublin Police Bill through its committee stage in the House of Commons, an announcement on the following day reported that 'the expedition which is to be commanded by General Sir Arthur Wellesley is not yet in a sufficient state of readiness, and that gallant officer will not leave town for a few days.'[15] Meantime, in case French agents had failed to see the Cork papers of 8th June, the *Morning Chronicle* reprinted their accurate account of the force collected in that city.

On 15th June, the Peninsular war first came before Parliament. Richard Brinsley Sheridan, despite the advice of his friends, insisted on calling attention to the affairs in Spain in a House which was trying to pass a vote of credit of £9,159 for the support of Protestant clergy in Ireland. Having scored a few party and personal points off Canning, he said that 'he did not ask Ministers to embark on any foolish or romantic speculation;

28

but he was satisfied there never was such a time, since the commencement of the French Revolution – taking it for granted that the flame would spread – there never was so great an opportunity and occasion for this country to strike a bold stroke, which might in the end rescue the world. He confessed he was not friendly to ministers; but this was not a subject for party. He, therefore, wished to express his opinion to ministers, and that opinion was, that they should not deal in dribblets; but if they could not do much they should do nothing. Let Spain see that we were not inclined to stint the services we had in our power to render to her – that we were not actuated by the desire for any petty advantage to ourselves; but that our exertions were to be solely directed to the attainment of the grand and general object – the emancipation of the world.'[16] Canning replied in suitable terms saying that 'No interest can be so purely British as Spanish success: no conquest so advantageous to England as conquering from France the complete integrity of the Spanish dominions in every quarter of the globe.' A French emigré newspaper, which was clearly unused to British politics, wrote that 'the spirit of party is mute; the most inveterate hatreds extinct; enthusiasm has banished the spirit of opposition; the walls of Westminster are astonished at seeing for the first time, a perfect unity of sentiments, words and actions.' More realistically an opposition paper wrote, 'The short altercation which took place in the House of Commons on Wednesday night has had the effect of expressing in unequivocal terms the interest which the nation takes in the struggle; and in so far it is favourable to the glorious cause. At nine o'clock last night General Sir Arthur Wellesley left his house in Harley Street to proceed from thence to Holyhead . . . to join the expedition that is fitting out [at Cork] for the assistance of the Spaniards.'[17]

Meanwhile deputies from other provinces of Spain were reaching England. They were received with acclaim. 'On Saturday night the Spanish club gave a splendid entertainment at the City of London Tavern to the Patriotic Deputies and other Spanish gentlemen at present in town. Six turtles were dressed for the occasion.'[18] Ten days later 'the Earl Camden [Lord President of the Council] gave a great Turtle feast at his house in Arlington Street. The Visconde de Materosa, his patriotic coadjutors and his secretary were of the company, and the greater part of the Ministry.' The following night the Spaniards partook of the 'splendid hospitality of Lord Mulgrave at his house at the Admiralty' and on the day following they had a 'most sumptuous dinner at the house of Mr. Secretary Canning.' But meanwhile the Opposition which, after fifteen years of war, had found a plan of which it could approve and would not understand that amphibious operations took time to mount, was getting restive. On 18th June the *Morning Chronicle* remarked: 'We do not say that our Ministers have been idle, but we certainly have not had any public proof of their activity.' By 17th July they were attacking Castlereagh for not having got the expedition under way. 'It does not appear that the expedition has sailed from Cork at the date of the latest advices from that port. The professional zeal and alacrity of Sir Arthur Wellesley are too well known to permit of a suspicion being entertained in the mind of any man of his being the cause of the delay. It is more probable that the delay rests with ministers and that it proceeds either from some doubt as to what ought to be the destination of the armament, or from indecision in the choice of the person who is eventually to have the command of it. Lord Castlereagh boasts mightily, and on every occasion, of the vigour and dispatch with which the business of his department is conducted; but as happens to all great boasters, his performance generally keeps at a very respectful distance from his promise. Indeed, if his instructions are written in the same extraordinary style in which he delivers his speeches in Parliament, he should publish a grammar and dictionary of his own, for the purpose of enabling general officers to understand the orders with the execution of which they are entrusted. . . . We should not be at all astonished if it should turn out that Sir A. Wellesley has been waiting in Dublin for an explanation of the instructions which he received before, or more probably, since his departure from London.'

Moreover, the idea of launching small sea-borne armies magically to effect great feats of liberation had seized the minds of the

Whigs both in Parliament and the Press. 'Never was a moment so favourable to display to advantage the peculiar character of our strength. It was the constant sentiment of the late Lord Nelson, that we had never put forth the real energies of England. It was his plan to have an army *afloat* – that is, an army embarked in transports, accompanied by a fleet of men of war, to hover on the coasts of the enemy, and in such a moment as the present to harass his troops incessantly, by drawing them from one part of his empire to another. On the coast of Italy, for instance, what might not be done by a hovering army? The Italians must be ready to rise when the accounts from Spain shall reach them, and a hovering army of only 20,000 men might rescue all the kingdoms of Italy from the rod of the tryrant.'[19]

The government, which suffered from being confined to the realities of time and space and which had at least some knowledge of military practicalities, plodded on. They did publicly clear up one small anomaly. On 5th July the *London Gazette* announced that 'His Majesty having taken into his consideration the exertions of the Spanish nation for the deliverance of their country from the tyranny and usurpation of France, and the assurance which His Majesty has received from several of the provinces of Spain, of their friendly disposition towards this kingdom; His Majesty is pleased, by and with the advice of his Privy Council, to order, and it is hereby ordered that all hostilities on the part of His Majesty shall cease.'

References

(The key to the abbreviations used in the references will be found in the Bibliography on page 202.)

Chapter 1. 'Two Spanish Noblemen'

1 MC 6 June '08
2 ib
3 Watson. 444
4 Jourdan. 9
5 SD vi 80. Undated memorandum by AW

6 **HD 4**
7 ib 13
8 ib 12
9 ib 17
10 ib 152. Castlereagh to HD, 25 May 'o8
11 Cintra 250. The Representatives of the Principality of Asturias to King George III, 25 May '08
12 MC 9 June '08
13 Cintra 251. Canning to Representative of the Principality of the Asturias, 12 June '08
14 MC 10 June '08
15 MC 11 June '08
16 MC 16 June '08
17 MC 17 June '08
18 MC 27 June '08
19 MC 5 July '08

SPAIN AND PORTUGAL IN 1808

c

'A Particular Service'

THE government had decided to send troops to Spain about a week before the Asturian deputies arrived in London. These, it is to be presumed, were to be the 10,000 men supposedly requested by General Castaños at Gibraltar. They had also appointed a commander, Sir Arthur Wellesley, Chief Secretary for Ireland. On 4th June, four days before the deputies landed, he wrote to his chief, the Lord-Lieutenant, that 'the government have lately been talking to me about taking the command of the corps destined for Spain, which is to be assembled at Cork, but nothing is yet settled about it.'[1]

It is important to distinguish between Lieutenant-General Sir Arthur Wellesley as he was at this time and the later legend-encrusted image of Field-Marshal the Duke of Wellington, the father-figure of early Victorian England. In the summer of 1808 he was thirty-nine, a lean, wiry figure of about five foot ten – his most pronounced feature being a sharp, prominent nose, although even that was not the dominant characteristic so familiar from his portraits in old age. He was an Anglo-Irishman from the Protestant Ascendancy, the younger son of an ineffectual Irish earl and a formidable mother. In his days at Eton, curtailed through lack of funds, he was noted more for dreaminess than for attention to his studies. From his father he had inherited a modest talent for the violin, and his contemporaries at Eton had noted, with surprise, that he was competent at fisticuffs. A spell on the continent had given him polished manners and fluent French. He had charm, a kindly nature, somewhat obscured by a shyness which made him abrupt with strangers, a keen sense of humour and, on occasions, a vivid Irish temper. His mother compared him unfavourably to his brilliant eldest brother, the 2nd Earl of Mornington (later Marquess of Wellesley) and saw no future for him except in the army. 'He is food for powder and nothing else.'

He joined the army at the age of seventeen as an ensign in an unfashionable regiment. Six years later he was a captain of Light Dragoons having, in the vagaries of promotion by purchase, been on the books of six regiments and having served with none of them. His military service up to 1793 had been, almost entirely, as an aide-de-camp at Viceregal Lodge in Dublin.

As soon as war was declared, Wellesley took seriously to soldiering. With the help of his brother, he purchased first a majority, then the lieutenant-colonelcy of the Thirty Third Foot, which he transformed into one of the finest regiments in the

Line. In the Flanders campaign of 1793–95, perhaps the nadir of the history of British arms, Wellesley was one of the few British officers to gain distinction and three years later he arrived with his regiment in India. There he won real distinction as a commander and as an administrator, both civil and military. He returned to England in 1805 with two major victories, Assaye and Argaum, to his credit, a major-general and a Knight of the Bath. More important to his future career he had learned, from the rigours of campaigning in India, an understanding and a mastery of logistics which none of his contemporaries could match.

On his return, England could offer him little, only the command of an under-strength brigade at Hastings. He entered Parliament through a pocket borough largely to defend the reputation of his brother, then Governor-General of India, who was under vicious attack from the less reputable parts of the East India Company lobby. Party politics he detested. 'I am no party man', he wrote to John Moore and, although he was associated 'in friendship with many of those persons who are now at the head of affairs',[2] his first seat in Parliament had been given him by a Whig. Nevertheless, his excellent judgment and his skill as an administrator, attracted the attention of ministers to him. William Pitt, shortly before his death remarked 'Sir Arthur Wellesley is unlike all other military men with whom I have conversed. He never makes a difficulty or hides his ignorance in vague generalities. If I put a question to him, he answers it distinctly; if I want an explanation, he gives it clearly; if I desire an opinion, I get from him one supported by reasons which are always sound. He is a very remarkable man.' Lord Castlereagh, Secretary of State for War, was an old friend from Dublin days and sought his advice on military problems. In 1807, Sir Arthur was made Chief Secretary for Ireland, the effective head of the Irish government, with a seat in the cabinet.

Competently as he discharged the frequently distasteful task of governing Ireland, he was essentially a soldier – a thorough-going professional soldier at a time when the British Army was more noted for amateurism, of a more or less inspired nature, than for serious attention to military studies. This and his Indian successes made him a suspect figure to the higher reaches of the military hierarchy. He was young, competent and involved in politics – everything that least appealed to the older generation of British generals. Far from being the reactionary arch-conservative that our great-grandfathers remembered with awe, his military contemporaries regarded him as a pushing young man with dangerously unorthodox views who was likely to use his political connections to gratify his military ambitions.

From the start, many generals regarded Wellesley's appointment to the command of the expeditionary force as a political job, not least since the Wellesleys and their adherents formed an important section of the Government's supporters in Parliament. This, however, was the least of the general's worries. The British military system might well have been devised to make the mounting of overseas operations difficult, control being in the hands of numerous independent officials and bodies with behind them a long tradition of defective co-operation. As Secretary for War, Lord Castlereagh had the responsibility for deciding the destination of all expeditionary forces and of recommending the name of the commander to the King. All dealings with the Spaniards, however, had to be conducted by Canning, as Foreign Secretary, and even if Castlereagh and Canning had been on better terms there must inevitably have been frictions from the conflicting demands of military and foreign policy. Canning did not neglect his opportunities for advising and criticising. The administrative business of getting together a force of infantry and cavalry was the task of the Secretary at War, a junior minister whose office was quite distinct from Castlereagh's, and who alone could authorise the movement of troops within Britain. For troops in Ireland, application had to be made to the Lord-Lieutenant. To provide Artillery and Engineers, together with ammunition, weapons, camp equipment and, if any existed, maps, was the task of the Master-General of the Ordnance, Lord Chatham, a member of the cabinet who in this instance was angling for the command of the expedition for himself. The Commander-in-Chief, at the Horse Guards, had to appoint subordinate commanders above the rank of colonel and all members of the staff. All questions of land transport and the supply of food, fuel and forage were the responsibility of the Treasury, which also had to supply the Paymasters-General with sufficient specie for the expedition to pay its way. Troop transports had to be secured from the Transport Office, a semi-independent offshoot of the Admiralty and Their Lordships of the Admiralty, who preserved a fierce independence from the Secretary for War, had to agree to provide men-of-war for convoy duty. The arrangements for the supply of medical services came under a Board of archaic constitution and striking inefficiency. In the circumstances it was little short of miraculous that Wellesley's expedition got under way as soon as it did.

Wellesley's immediate command consisted of the troops at Cork and Spencer's brigade at Gibraltar. The first consisted of seven and a half strong battalions of infantry, 6,924 rank and file, together with a Royal Veteran Battalion of 750 men, 'a good corps, but the soldiers being old and disabled by wounds and otherwise for active service, cannot march.'[3] To these were joined two weak battalions* stationed nearby and a regiment of light dragoons which, with two batteries of artillery, had to be sailed round from Portsmouth. Spencer's brigade, which Dalrymple, on his own initiative made up with a strong battalion and three batteries,† amounted to five battalions, 4,793 rank and file. Orders were sent to Madeira for a further battalion to join the force but this did not arrive until the fighting was over.

The largest reinforcement that could be looked for was Moore's force of one regiment and eleven battalions (in all 10,864 men), if they could be brought back from Gothenburg. In the meanwhile, the only troops immediately available were the two brigades from eastern England, little more than 4,000 bayonets altogether. By scraping the garrisons of England and Ireland it would be

* These battalions, the 36th and 1/45th were only 589 and 500 strong respectively compared to the original battalions at Cork which numbered between 875 and 987.
† No horse could be sent with these guns as no horse transports were available.

38

possible to send overseas by September four regiments of hussars and ten battalions of infantry (including two of the Foot Guards).

All going well, therefore, it should be possible to send to the Peninsula rather more than 13,000 men as soon as they could be found transports; a first reinforcement, almost immediately, of 4,000, followed by 11,000 more as soon as Moore could be disentangled from the Baltic. By the autumn, the force should have a strength of 44,000 rank and file.

There remained the most difficult problem of all – the destination of this large armament. The news coming out of Spain was so fragmented and contradictory that it was hard to see where Britain could best play a part. All that was apparent was that the provincial Juntas, with a unanimity which marked none of their other proceedings, asserted through their delegates that they did not want British troops. Money and arms they requested and were supplied with in large amounts. It was wounding to the British national pride that, at a time when, with a unity that had not been felt since the war began, they had decided to help Spain the Spaniards resolutely rejected military help.

The possible exception was the 'Supreme' Junta of Seville. Since the secretary to General Castaños had mentioned, almost in an aside to Dalrymple, that 10,000 British troops would be required in the field, ministers could not be certain whether they had not been committed to providing that number. Meanwhile, the Spaniards never reverted to the request and continued to refuse Spencer's brigade permission to land at Cadiz. It was not until the second week in August when news reached London that Castaños had defeated a French army at Bailen on 19th July, and had forced it to capitulate that the possibility of a corps of 10,000 men being required in southern Spain could finally be abandoned. The victory at Bailen, if anything, strengthened the Spanish reluctance to accept military help and made them even more confident that they could eject the French by their own efforts. It was unfortunate for them that they never won another major action until 1813.

There was one over-riding necessity for the choice of a destination – there must be a deep water, all-weather harbour, which could be used as a base. This meant, in fact, that if the army was to go to Spain, it must go to either Ferrol, Vigo or Cadiz, but the deputies of Galicia had already firmly stated that they did not want British troops at Ferrol or Vigo and, although no such statement had been made from Seville with regard to Cadiz, Spencer's corps had already been turned away from that city. Two possibilities remained, Gibraltar, which was even further than Cadiz from the scene of the fighting, and Lisbon.

The Portuguese insurrection against the French was much later than that in Spain, and was, indeed, set off by the division of Spanish troops which had been occupying Oporto and was recalled to Spain by the Galician Junta. It was not until the third week in June that a Supreme Junta of the Kingdom was established in Oporto, under the Bishop of that city, and although rumours of disturbances in Portugal were current in London in the early part of July it was not until the middle of the month that definite news of the Portuguese rising and requests for help reached England. The politicians, Press and public were singularly unenthusiastic about helping the Portuguese, such assistance seeming to detract from the national effort, which had assumed the character of a crusade, to assist Spain. Moreover, the Portuguese were in poor shape to assist themselves. The Portuguese army had not been an effective force for many years, and the better parts of it had been marched off to Germany to serve Napoleon in the previous year. The remainder had been disbanded. At most the Junta in Oporto could lay its hands on 5,000 muskets and a dozen light field pieces, while it was thought in London that the French army of occupation was at least 26,000 strong. The eventual decision to land the British army in Portugal was largely a naval affair, almost in despite of the wishes of ministers and public opinion. Lisbon had the safest and largest harbour in the Peninsula. It would serve admirably as an entry port for an army fighting in Portugal and western Spain and as an invaluable base for the Royal Navy in its blockading tasks. Moreover it contained an irresistible bait for the navy – nine Russian ships of the line and a frigate which, since Russia was at peace with Portugal, were enjoying the security of a neutral port, safe from the English with whom they were at war. The decision was probably clinched by a letter from Sir Charles Cotton, the admiral commanding the British squadron off the Tagus, dated 12th June, which stated that 'from every account I have been able to procure, there are not more than 4,000 troops in Lisbon, from whom the Spaniards are now completely separated, and against whom the populace was highly incensed; so that I feel it my duty to state to their lordships my opinion, that five or six thousand British troops might affect a landing, gain possession of the forts on the Tagus, and by co-operating with His Majesty's fleet, give to our possession the whole of the maritime means now collected in the Tagus.'[4]

This was wholly misleading information. Even Lord Collingwood, commanding the Mediterranean fleet, gave it as his opinion that 'reports received in the way Sir Charles Cotton got his information, should not have much confidence in the truth of them'[5] and, in fact, at the time that Cotton wrote there were not less than 15,000 French troops in the immediate vicinity of Lisbon. The results, however, were wholly beneficial. It was this report that finally tipped the balance in favour of sending the expeditionary force to Portugal. The experience of the next two years was to show that if the British force had gone, as was originally intended, to act as auxiliaries to the Spaniards, not all their bravery and discipline, nor the skill of Wellesley or Moore could have saved them from total disaster. This, however, was not the public view. The Parliamentary Opposition continued to maintain that the army should have gone to Spain and as late as February 1810 the Secretary for War could still write to Lord Wellington, as he then was, that 'there is no doubt that in this country a higher value is set upon Cadiz than upon Lisbon.'[6]

*　　*　　*

Wellesley got his first instructions from the Commander-in-Chief on 14th June. These merely appointed him to command the troops waiting at Cork and Gibraltar 'to be employed upon a particular service' and to instruct him 'to take the earliest opportunity to assume the command of this force, and carry into effect such instructions as you may receive from His Majesty's Ministers.'*[7] Two days later, on the eve of setting out for Ireland, he dined with Mr. Croker, to whom he was handing over the London end of his job as Chief Secretary. 'After dinner', wrote his host, 'we were alone and talked over our business. There was one point of the Dublin Pipe Water Bill on which I differed a little from him. At last I said, perhaps he would reconsider the subject, and write to me from Dublin about it. He said in his quick way, "No, no, I shall be no wiser tomorrow than I am today. I have given you my reasons: you must decide for yourself." When this was over, and I was making some memoranda on the papers, he seemed to lapse into a kind of reverie, and remained silent so long that I asked him what he was thinking of. He replied, "Why, to say the truth, I am thinking of the French I am going to fight. I have not seen them since the campaign in Flanders, and a dozen years of victory under Bonaparte must have made them better still. They have besides, it seems, a new system of strategy,† which has out-manœuvred and overwhelmed all the armies of Europe. 'Tis enough to make one thoughtful; but no matter; my die is cast, they may overwhelm me, but I don't think they will out-manœuvre me. First, because I am not afraid of them, as every one else seems to be; and secondly, because if what I hear of their system of manœuvres be true, I think it a false one against steady troops. I suspect all the continental armies were more than half beaten before the battle was begun. I, at least, will not be frightened beforehand." '[8]

At Holyhead the wind was adverse and it was not until the afternoon of 20th June that he reached Dublin. While he handed over his Irish duties, he started to take over the troops in their

* Wellesley remained one of H.M. Ministers throughout the campaign, and continued to draw the salary of Chief Secretary. There was no objection to this practice as long as he was successful.

† See p. 108–10

transports at Cork. His first care was for their health and he wrote to his friend, Major-General Rowland Hill, who had been commanding them pending his appointment, 'I have to request that you will make arrangements with the agent of transports, that the soldiers embarked may have fresh provisions and vegetables every day. . . . I also think it very desirable that the soldiers should have permission to go ashore as they may wish, under such regulations as you may think proper; and that the regiments should be sent ashore and exercised in their turns.'[9] 'It will tend much to the health of the men, and will make them feel less unpleasantly the heat and confinement of the transports.'[10]

It had originally been planned that the cavalry and artillery, sailing from ports in the south of England, should meet Wellesley's fleet off the coast of Spain. Now there was delay in the issue of his orders and it was decided that the whole should rendezvous at Cork. The reasons for this delay came to him in a letter from Castlereagh, written on 21st June. 'Our accounts from Cadiz are bad; no disposition there or in the neighbourhood of Gibraltar to move; General Spencer returning to Gibraltar. . . . The cabinet are desirous of postponing, till they hear again, their final issue on your instructions, being unwilling you should get too far to the southward, whilst the spirit of exertion appears to reside more to the northward.'[11]

Immediately on receipt of this Wellesley applied to Castlereagh's office for permission to land the troops since they were 'certainly too much crowded'[12] but this permission does not appear to have been forthcoming. It would have been a wise precaution since it was not until 3rd July that he received, in Dublin, his orders and even then the contingent from England had not arrived at Cork. Meanwhile, the troops, apart from being landed for exercise, continued in their foetid transports, although the officers were allowed on shore and spent their time 'amusing themselves in perfect idleness, though very gaily. . . . We had a gay ball here yesterday, in a storehouse fitted up with flags, for the relief of the distressed soldiers' wives. We had a good many people, and collected about £50 free of expenses, little enough among so many objects.'[13] Enthusiasm for sailing to the Peninsula was high. One officer wrote: 'I do not know anything in the world that gives me so much joy as the idea of going amongst the Spaniards. It is the finest cause we can be engaged in.'[14] While another, born in Portugal, the son of one of the great Oporto British wine dynasties, shared the enthusiasm but took the optimistic line that was prevalent in the Press. 'I am for going to Spain. It is a noble service assisting a nation fighting for its independence, and it is impossible to say what a brave people fighting for liberty, and actuated at the same time by resentment for great injuries, and a bigoted attachment to ancient customs may do, if properly supported. At all events, our assisting the independence to the utmost of our power the mother country will greatly facilitate our establishing the independence of [Latin] America, whither I hope will be our ultimate destination.'[15]

Wellesley's orders reflected the lack of definite information from which London was suffering at the end of June. All that was known for certain was that there was rebellion against the French in many parts of Spain, but that Galicia and Asturias, where 'the spirit of exertion appears to reside', were quite firm in refusing British troops. 'As the deputies from the above provinces do not desire the employment of any corps of His Majesty's troops in the quarter of Spain from which they are immediately delegated; but have rather pressed, as calculated to operate a powerful diversion in their power, the importance of directing the efforts of the British troops to the expulsion of the enemy from Portugal, that the insurrection against the French may therefore become general throughout that kingdom as well as Spain, it is therefore deemed expedient that your attention should be immediately directed to that object.'[16]

This was no order to go to Portugal. Even in the terms of elaborate courtesy in which the orders of those days were dressed, to 'deem it expedient' that a general's attention should be drawn to a place did not constitute a definite instruction. A later paragraph laid down that, 'in the rapid succession in which events must be expected to follow each other, situated as Spain and Portugal now are, much must be left to your judgment and decision on the spot. His Majesty is graciously pleased to confide to you the fullest discretion to act according to circumstances for the benefit of his service; and you may rely on your measures being favourably interpreted, and receiving the most cordial support.'[17] Furthermore, the Government's wish to intervene in Spain rather than Portugal was further stressed by an instruction to Sir Arthur to precede his convoy in 'a fast-sailing frigate' to Coruña 'where you will have the best means of learning the actual state of things in Spain and Portugal.' If, after consultations in Coruña, it appeared that the Portuguese suggestion was impractical, the general was to seek permission of the Junta of Galicia to put into Vigo, there to await reinforcements and, by implication, new orders.

As soon as Castlereagh had sealed these orders up, he received Sir Charles Cotton's letter of 12th June (*see p.* 41) with the estimate that there were 'not more than 4,000 [French] troops in Lisbon.' This he immediately forwarded to Wellesley, writing in his covering letter that 'you will, of course, feel it of the most pressing importance that your armament should proceed off the Tagus . . . with the least possible delay.'[18] He also suggested that Wellesley should not go, himself, to Coruña but that he should send 'a confidential officer to that port' who, after consulting with the Junta should 'meet you off Cape Finisterre,* or follow you to the Tagus.'[19] This last instruction Wellesley felt compelled to refuse as 'I rather think that . . . I shall best serve the cause by going myself to Coruña.'[20]

Wellesley's instructions were, therefore, not specific, even as modified after the receipt of Cotton's letter. Government, Opposition, Press, people and his own army wanted him to go to Spain. The Government had come to the reluctant conclusion that this was, probably, impractical and had given him strong suggestions that Portugal would be a more profitable destination. The final decision was left to him.

One thing in the instructions was made perfectly clear.

---

* Cape Finisterre in this connection is the cape of that name at the north-western corner of Spain rather than the department of Brittany.

Wellesley's aim was to be 'The entire and absolute evacuation of the Peninsula, by the troops of France, being, after what has lately passed, the only security for Spanish independence, and the only basis upon which the Spanish nation should be prevailed upon to treat or to lay down their arms.'[21] The Portuguese nation and their independence were not mentioned.

'The entire and absolute evacuation of the Peninsula, by the troops of France' was a sizeable task to entrust to an expeditionary force whose embarkation strength, omitting the 750 Veterans, was 9,738 men of all ranks. In addition to this Spencer's 5,000 men had been put under Wellesley's command but Castlereagh's orders for Spencer to join Wellesley were conditional. He was instructed not to join if 'your corps should be engaged on any service more to the southward, which in your judgment it is of importance to His Majesty's interests should not be abandoned.'[22] Since London had had no reports from Gibraltar dated less than three weeks earlier, Spencer's junction with Wellesley could be by no means certain.

There was no reliable estimate of the French strength in Spain and Portugal, and although their actual strength of 165,000 (August) could not have been known, no realistic estimate of the troops which Napoleon would have considered necessary for an undertaking as large as the military domination of the Peninsula could have come to a figure very much smaller.

Wellesley's force was, as far as the infantry went, a very good one for its numbers. All the line infantry were from first battalions and six of the eight line battalions were very strong. There were also fourteen companies of riflemen, a very high proportion of skilled light troops for that time. All this even in the two weak line battalions, was infantry of the highest class, with all the disciplined toughness that made British infantry incomparable at that time. The other arms were not so well represented. For cavalry there were only 381 all ranks of the Twentieth Light Dragoons. These were well trained horsemen but would have been an insufficient contingent even if they had all been mounted but only 180 horses could be shipped. Two batteries of artillery accompanied the expedition, but the Ordnance Board provided no horses since 'it was very uncertain that the troops would ever land in Spain, and it was thought the horses of the artillery might suffer, and might be lost to the service by being kept so long in the transports.'[23] Instead, the artillery was provided with horses from the Irish commissariat, which the senior artillery officer with Wellesley described as 'old, blind, and casts from cavalry.'[24] Engineers were represented by six officers, one sergeant, and eleven other ranks.

Transport and supply had been totally neglected until Wellesley took command of the expedition. To save time two Assistant Commissaries were taken from the Irish establishment, and to assist with the problems of transport the personnel of two companies from the Irish corps of Waggoners were embarked, although they could not take their waggons with them. To secure even these modest but essential adjuncts to his force, Wellesley had to make full use of his position as Chief Secretary and to commence his letters on the subject 'I have it in command from the Lord-Lieutenant'. Without this local influence it seems likely that no arrangements for transport and supply would have been made. As it was, the only wheeled vehicles which could be taken by the expedition were, apart from gun carriages and limbers for the twelve guns, four camp equipment waggons and three forge carts.

This was perhaps some slight improvement on the situation seven years previously when, after the Egyptian campaign of 1801, Sir John Moore had angrily remarked, 'The military operations of Great Britain have been designed by ministers ignorant of military affairs, and too arrogant and self-sufficient to consult military men. Sir Ralph Abercromby, when he received his orders at Gibraltar to attack Egypt, had from 14,000 to 15,000 infantry and artillery, 250 dismounted cavalry, not a horse for either cavalry or artillery, not a waggon or the means of conveying an article a yard from the beach.'[25] At least now there were a few troop horses, seven carts and three hundred draught animals, old though they might be. Castlereagh justified the shortcomings, which were more on the part of the Treasury and the Ordnance Office, than of his own office, on the grounds that 'the great delay and expense that would attend embarking and sending from hence all those means which would be requisite to render the army completely moveable immediately on its landing, has determined His Majesty's government to trust in a great measure to the resources of the country for their supplies.'[26] This may have sounded convincing in Whitehall, and to the taxpayer, but it was cold comfort to a general who might have to fight an action as soon as he landed. Wellesley made his views perfectly clear in a letter to Castlereagh before he left Dublin to join his command. 'I declare that I do not understand the principles on which our military establishments are formed if, when large corps of troops are sent out to perform important and difficult services, they are not to have with them those means of equipment which they require and which the establishment can afford, such as horses to draw artillery and drivers attached to the Commissariat, when these means are not wanted at home; and what is more, considering the number of horses and drivers in England, all of whom the public could command in case of emergency, never can be wanted excepting for foreign service.'[27]

Having delivered himself of this broadside and received his orders, Wellesley rode down to Cork in the hope of being able to put to sea immediately he arrived on 6th July, only to find 'the 20th Light Dragoons and 3,000 tons of shipping for the infantry are not arrived.'[28] There were other deficiencies which had to be rectified. The Irish establishment had reluctantly parted with the two companies of Waggoners but had omitted to provide them with equipment, even a blanket; no hospital ship had arrived and 'the camp kettles provided for the use of my force are of the Flanders pattern, the size of which would cause considerable inconvenience in the service in which it is probable I shall be engaged.'[29]

At last, on the 10th, all the troops were assembled and embarked but he had to write to Castlereagh 'The wind is still contrary, but we hope it will change this evening. We are unmoored, and shall not wait one moment after the wind shall be fair. I see that people in England complain of the delay which has taken place in the sailing of the expedition; but in fact none has taken place; and even if all had been on board we could not have sailed before this day. With all the expedition which we could use, we could not get the horses of the artillery to Cork before yesterday; and it was only yesterday that the 20th dragoons arrived, and the ships to contain the 36th and a detachment of the 45th, which arrived yesterday and embarked.'[30]

It was not until 12th June that the wind changed and, as a sergeant of dragoons wrote, 'a magnificent squadron put to sea, amid the cheers of the troops, the playing of the bands, and in a state of weather which held out every promise of an agreeable voyage.'[31] As soon as the fleet had cleared the coast of Ireland, Wellesley transferred to the frigate *Crocodile* and, crowding on all sail, made for Coruña.

References

Chapter 2. 'A Particular Service'

1 SD v 444. AW to Richmond, 4 June '08
2 WD iv 157. AW to Moore, 17 Sept '08
3 SD vi 103. AW to Cotton, 8 Aug '08
4 Cintra 257. Cotton to Pole, 12 June '08
5 HD 233. Collingwood to HD, 23 June '08
6 SD vi 484. Liverpool to AW, 14 June '10
7 WD iv 10. Duke of York to AW, 14 June '08
8 Croker i 13
9 WD iv 15. AW to Hill, 25 June '08
10 WD iv 16. AW to Hill, 29 June '08
11 WD iv 13. Castlereagh to AW, 21 June '08
12 WD iv 15. AW to Charles Stewart, 25 June '08
13 Warre 8 & 15
14 Gomm 99
15 Warre 15
16 WD iv 17. Castlereagh to AW, 30 June '08
17 ib 16
18 ib 20
19 ib
20 WD iv 24. AW to Castlereagh, 7 July '08
21 WD iv 19. Castlereagh to AW, 30 June '08
22 Cintra 252. Castlereagh to Spencer, 30 June '08

23 Cintra 50. AW's evidence
24 Duncan ii 58. Robe to Macleod, 7 Aug '08
25 Moore Diary ii 58
26 WD iv 29. Castlereagh to AW, 15 July '08
27 SD vi 87. AW to Castlereagh, 29 July '08
28 WD iv 24. AW to Castlereagh, 7 July '08
29 WD iv 25. AW to Floyd, 8 July '08
30 WD iv 26. AW to Castlereagh, 10 July '08
31 Hussar i 247

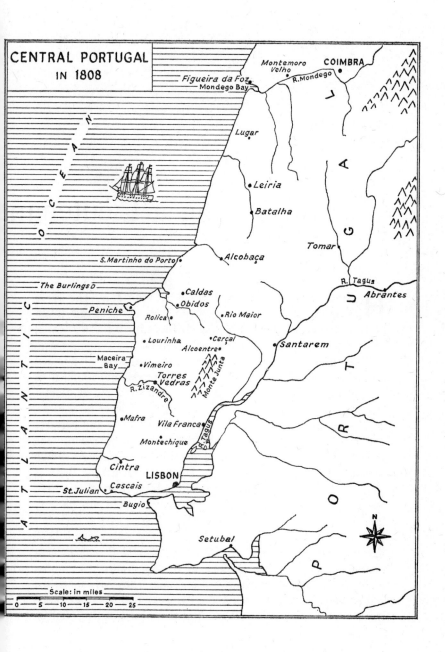

CENTRAL PORTUGAL
IN 1808

O C E A N

A T L A N T I C

Figueira da Foz
Mondego Bay
Montemoro Velho
COIMBRA
R.Mondego

Lugar

Leiria

Batalha

Tomar

S.Martinho do Porto

Alcobaça

R. Tagus
Abrantes

The Burlings

Caldas

Obidos

Rio Maior

Peniche

Rolica

Lourinha

Cerçal
Alcoentre

Santarem

Maceira Bay

Vimeiro

Torres Vedras

R.Zizandre

Monte Junta

Mafra

Vila Franca

Montechique

R.Tagus

Cintra

LISBON

St.Julian

Cascais

Bugio

Setubal

L

U

G

A

L

P

O

R

T

Scale: in miles

0 — 5 — 10 — 15 — 20 — 25

N

'So Young a Lieutenant

H.M.S. *Crocodile* reached Coruña on 20th July. The Junta and the townsfolk were delighted at this concrete token of British support. After his first visit ashore, Wellesley wrote, 'they manifested the greatest satisfaction upon our arrival, received us with the utmost civility and cordiality, illuminated the town at night, and the whole of the inhabitants attended us to our boat when we returned on board the frigate at night.'[1] His first impressions of the situation in Spain were favourable. 'The whole of Spain, with the exception of Biscay and Navarre and the neighbourhood of Madrid, is in arms against the French. . . . It is impossible to describe the sentiment which prevails throughout the country. I am informed that there is no such thing as a French party; and indeed, from what I have seen of the town, I should imagine that it could not be very safe for any man to declare himself in favour of the French.'[2] The military situation seemed, for the most part, sound. 'The Spaniards have defeated and destroyed several French detachments: viz. one under Dupont to the southward, one under Lefebvre in Aragon, and two in Catalonia. They have taken the fort of Figueras, near Rosas in the Pyrenees, and have blockaded the French troops in Barcelona. But the great army of Galicia, eneral'

consisting of 50,000 men, received a check on the 14th of this month from a French corps under Marshal Bessières. The French had not more than half that number, and lost about 7,000 men. . . . The Spaniards lost two pieces of Cannon, the French six; the Spanish army retreated about twenty miles towards this province.'[3] 'These accounts . . . although credited, are only private; but I credit them.'[4]

Although Wellesley as yet unversed in the interpretation of Spanish military intelligence, gave credit to these accounts, they painted a wholly unrealistic picture of the scene. Only in Valencia had the French suffered any serious reverse,* although there had been minor repulses in Catalonia and Aragon. Figueras, the vital fortress commanding the road from France to Barcelona, was still in French hands and the blockade of Barcelona was little more than an irritant to the garrison. Worst of all, the 'check' which the Army of Galicia was reported to have suffered was, in fact a serious defeat. The combined armies of Galicia and Castile, 22,000 men, had been attacked at Medina de Rio Seco

* Dupont, in Andalusia had, in fact, been defeated the previous day, 19th July, but this news could not possibly have reached Coruña by any human means.

53

by 13,700 French under Marshal Bessières. The Spaniards, though many of them behaved with the greatest bravery, were utterly routed losing more than 2,000 in killed, wounded and prisoners apart from about 1,000 recruits who took the opportunity to desert. The French took ten guns and lost none of their own and their casualties were only 400. Following their defeat the Captains-General of Galicia and Castile had quarrelled bitterly and separated their armies, leaving the main road to Madrid unguarded. On the day that Wellesley arrived at Coruña, Joseph Bonaparte made a state entry into Madrid as King of Spain.

The watered-down account of their army's defeat at Medina de Rio Seco had certainly not had the effect of making the Junta of Galicia revise their views about their need for British troops. 'The check does not appear to have affected the spirits or to have diminished the hopes of the people here. They say that they do not require men, and have not asked me to give them any assistance.'[5] 'I think that this disinclination to receive the assistance of British troops is founded in a great degree on the objection to give the command of their troops to British officers.'[6] They continued to press for a British landing in Portugal, whither they had detached a small division of Galician troops to assist in the revolt of the northern provinces.

The information available of the situation in Portugal was not very full and no more reliable than that about Spain. 'I find', wrote Wellesley, 'that Junot has collected, it is supposed 12,000 men at Lisbon; and the French still hold Almeida, and other points with 3,000 more. The three northern provinces of Portugal are in a state of insurrection, and there is a Portuguese army at Oporto, to join which 2,000 Spanish troops have marched from Galicia. I understand there is a Spanish corps of 20,000 men at Almaraz on the Tagus which corps will impede the communication between Junot and the army at Madrid. . . . The Junta [of Galicia] express great anxiety respecting my operations in Portugal, and have strongly recommended me not to attempt to land at Lisbon, or in the neighbourhood of the French army. They urge as an objection to this measure that I shall thereby lose the advantage of the co-operation of the Spanish and Portuguese forces at Oporto . . . and they recommend that I should disembark at Vigo or Oporto, and bring the allies with me to Lisbon.'[7]

This cautious advice, wholly untypical of contemporary Spanish thinking, was well worth considering. There was no reliable news of Spencer, 'the accounts respecting his movements are so very vague', but according to a message, heard at second-hand from a passing British man-of-war, he 'had gone to Ayamonte at the mouth of the Guadiana, to stop the progress of a French corps which was coming by that route from Portugal into Andalusia.' The Galicians had heard another story 'that 5,000 British troops had been in General Castaños' army, and had behaved remarkably well, but on what occasion and what troops, they did not know.'[8]

It seemed, therefore, that Wellesley with less than 10,000 men, might be invading Portugal in the face of a superior French force with no more support than 2,000 Galicians and a Portuguese army of which neither the numbers nor the state of training were known. On the evening of 21st July, the *Crocodile* put out from Coruña, for its rendezvous with the convoy off Cape Finisterre which it made on the following day. Telling them to follow, Wellesley and the frigate pushed southward to Oporto.

In Oporto, where he arrived on 24th July, Wellesley conferred with the Bishop, who was at the head of the local Junta, and found enthusiasm and very little else. 'The people are ready and desirous to take arms, but unfortunately there are none in the country.' At Oporto there were 1,500 Portuguese regulars, together with 500 Spanish infantry, a remnant of the occupation force. The 2,000 Galicians which he had expected to find had been stopped on the frontier 'because there were no orders at Braganza to allow it to enter the country.' The main Portuguese army had been sent forward to Coimbra; it was reported as consisting of 'a corps of about 5,000 men, regular troops and militia, including 300 cavalry, armed with 1,000 muskets got from the [British] fleet, fowling pieces &c., and 12,000 peasantry, mostly unarmed.'[9]

There was no news from Spencer except that he had been with the admiral off the mouth of the Tagus three weeks earlier, but

55

the admiral had sent a letter informing Wellesley that he had occupied the fort commanding the mouth of the Mondego at Figueira da Foz with 220 Marines, since 'that place I hold in view as very eligible for troops to debark at.'[10] He suggested that Wellesley, leaving the convoy to the northward, should sail down to the mouth of the Tagus for a consultation. This the general immediately did and on the 26th met Cotton and received from him a letter dated ten days earlier from Spencer, who at that time was ashore near Cadiz.

Spencer's letter was a depressing document. He declined to come north until he had obtained the permission of the Junta of Seville 'as I must presume the government would not wish the good harmony which at present exists, should be clouded by any act the Spaniards might interpret into a neglect of their interests.'[11] He added, however, that he had on 15th July sought the Junta's views on the subject. Almost more discouraging was a detailed breakdown 'obtained from some intelligent deserters, and from other channels,' and dated 21st June, of the French force in Portugal. This gave the total of Junot's force as 20,500 of whom 12,800 were either in Lisbon or at Setubal and on the south bank of the Tagus, within easy reach of the capital. A copy of this estimate had already been forwarded to London.

Wellesley was now in a position of great difficulty. There was no immediate prospect of Spencer joining him and the French force in Portugal was twice as strong as his own. It was clear that little if any help would be forthcoming from either the Spaniards or the Portuguese. On the other hand he had made a conditional offer to the Bishop of Oporto to disembark his troops at Figueira da Foz, to which port the Bishop had agreed to forward 500 mules 'of a description which could be applied either to draft or carriage,' and 150 horses for the dismounted troopers of the Light Dragoons, 'if I should determine to disembark the army at Mondego Bay.'[12] Moreover, public opinion in England was demanding that ministers should do something to help the Spaniards, and, since the Spaniards declined to accept direct military help, it was only by defeating the French in Portugal that the British army could assist.

56

Wellesley was always a man of quick and bold decision. He decided that he would land his army at Figueira and, in his words of five years later, 'to get in fortune's way'. He wrote to Spencer, stating, with justified exaggeration, that his instructions 'positively direct me to make an attack on the French troops in the Tagus, if I should find the force under my command sufficient to enable me to make it,' and ordered him north unless he should be 'actually engaged' in 'active operations'.[13] That done, the *Crocodile* turned north for Mondego, where the convoy was collecting, and Sir Arthur turned to his writing desk to prepare the necessary orders for his exceedingly chancy venture.

First came a 'Memorandum for Disembarcation' laying down the order of brigades in which the force was to land, led by Fane's brigade consisting of the fourteen companies of Riflemen of the Sixtieth and Ninety-Fifth backed by the Forty-Fifth. For all the troops 'the haversacks and canteens now in the regimental stores are to be given out to the men. Tin camp kettles are to be issued from the Quartermaster-General's stores to the regiments. . . . The men are to land, each with one pair of shoes, besides those on them, combs, razor, and a brush, which are to be packed up in their great coats. The knapsacks to be left in the transports, and the baggage of the officers, excepting such light articles as are necessary for them. A careful serjeant to be left in the headquarter ship of each regiment, and a careful private man in each of the other ships, in charge of the baggage. . . . The men will land with three days' bread and two days' meat cooked. . . . Each soldier will have three good flints. . . . Three days' oats to be landed with each of the horses.'[14] Then there was a memorandum for the Commissaries making careful arrangements for supplies and the allocation of the mules from Oporto. 'Besides the quantity of bread to be carried by the men themselves, a quantity, equal to three days' consumption for 10,000 men, must be carried, if possible on the backs of mules: viz. two bags, or 224 lb. on each mule; this will require 130 mules. . . . The medical department will require two carts to march with the army, carrying twenty-four bearers [i.e. stretchers] for wounded men, a case of utensils, and a medicine

57

chest.'[15] Next there was a joint proclamation signed by both Wellesley and Cotton to the People of Portugal telling them that 'the English soldiers, who land on your shore, do so with every sentiment of friendship, faith, and honour. The glorious struggle in which you are engaged is for all that is dear to man – the protection of your wives and children; the restoration of your lawful Prince; the independence, nay the very existence of your kingdom; and for the preservation of your holy religion.'[16] Finally, on the evening before the landing started, a long general order to the army, laying down the ration scales for the army and the procedure for requisitioning (in triplicate), and an exhortation that 'The troops are to understand that Portugal is a country friendly to His Majesty, that it is essentially necessary to their own success that the most strict obedience is preserved, that properties and persons should be respected, and that no injury should be done which it is possible to avoid. . . . It is almost essential to the success of the army that the religious prejudices and opinions of the people of the country should be respected. . . . When an officer or a soldier shall visit a church . . . he is to remain uncovered while in the church. When the Host passes in the streets, officers and soldiers, not on duty, are to halt and front it; the officers to pull off their hats, and the soldiers to put their hands to their caps. When it shall pass a guard, the guard will turn out and present arms.'[17]

The hard work of getting the orders out was relieved on 31st August by the first good news which had reached the expedition since it left England. Confirmed news arrived that the Spaniards under Castaños had beaten Dupont's army at Bailen, sixty miles east of Cordoba and forced it to surrender. Andalusia was free from the French: 'there can be nothing to detain General Spencer in that quarter.'[18]

Next day the troops began to go ashore and hardly had they started when a frigate sailed in bearing Captain Lord Burghersh, Third Dragoon Guards, with dispatches from Lord Castlereagh. It was, for Wellesley, the worst possible news. 'I am to acquaint you that His Majesty has been pleased to entrust the command of his troops serving on the coasts of Spain and Portugal to

Lieut.-General Sir Hew Dalrymple, with Lieut.-General Sir Harry Burrard, second in command.'[19] Other letters from Castlereagh told how the army was to be reinforced from England by 16,000 men and, apart from Dalrymple and Burrard, by four lieutenant-generals senior to Wellesley. The reinforced army was divided into divisions and brigades on orders from Whitehall, a most unusual proceeding, and the division which was allocated to Wellesley was to amount to seven battalions, four of which did not form part of his existing force.

Replying to Castlereagh Wellesley wrote with dignity: 'All I can say . . . is, that whether I am to command this army or not, or am to quit it, I shall do my best to ensure its success; and you may depend upon it that I shall not hurry the operations, or commence them one moment sooner than they ought to be commenced, in order that I may acquire the credit for the business.'[20] To the Lord Lieutenant of Ireland he wrote, 'I hope I shall have beaten Junot before any of them arrive, and then they may do as they please with me.'[21]

*   *   *

Castlereagh's letter to Wellesley had been dated 15th July – only three days after the convoy had sailed from Cork. In that short period two vital pieces of information had reached London, Spencer's report of 21st June (*see p.* 56) estimating Junot's strength in Portugal at over 20,000, more than four times Admiral Cotton's estimate on which the plans for Portugal had been built, and definite news that Moore's force from Sweden would be reaching England by about the middle of the month. Thus ministers were in the fortunate position of having a worthwhile requirement for troops and the ability to supply them. They decided to dispatch immediately the brigades of Acland and Anstruther which were already standing by in England and could leave in a few days* and to follow them with Moore's men as soon as they could be made ready to sail again.

These reinforcements brought the strength of the army destined

* They sailed on 19th July.

59

for Portugal to more than 30,000 with preparations going forward for the dispatch of 10,000 more. It was, therefore, impossible to leave the army in charge of an officer who was fourth from the bottom of the list of a hundred and thirty lieutenant-generals, to say nothing of two Field-Marshals and seventy generals. Wellesley, in any case, was only thirty-nine and his military reputation had been made largely in India. 'The Horse Guards', he said later, 'thought little of anyone who had served in India. An Indian victory was not only no ground for confidence, but it was actually grounds for suspicion.'[22] The fact that no other general on the list had victories of the magnitude of Assaye and Argaum to his credit did not affect the issue. The Duke of York's verdict that 'he is so young a lieutenant-general' summed up the general feeling and the fact that he was a member of a powerful and much disliked political family clinched the matter.

The government's problem was to know who to choose. Even Moore was only eighty-eighth on the list. In despair ministers turned to Dalrymple who was thirteenth in seniority.

Sir Hew Dalrymple was fifty-eight. He had been in the army since the age of thirteen but despite his forty-five years of service he had only seen one year of active service, when as a colonel he had commanded a composite battalion of grenadier companies at the battle of Farmars, and at the sieges of Valenciennes and Dunkirk in 1793. His early years had been passed in the infantry of the line but since 1790 he had been serving in the First Guards. His promotion had not been particularly rapid, it took him fifteen years to rise from ensign to lieutenant-colonel, a promotion Wellesley had achieved in six years and Lord Paget within a year, but Sir Hew was remarkable for neither wealth nor influence.†

Once a lieutenant-colonel, promotion came automatically and in 1794 he became a major-general, and seven years later a

† Sir Hew's great-uncle, the second Earl of Stair, who died three years before Dalrymple was born, had been a Field-Marshal, but by far his most distinguished relation was to be his nephew, Captain Hew Dalrymple Ross, R.H.A., who became famous as the Commander of the Chestnut Troop in the Peninsula and at Waterloo and, in 1868, a Field-Marshal.

lieutenant-general. Between his return from Flanders at the end of 1793, and his posting to Gibraltar in 1806, he had divided his time between the Northern Command at York and commanding, as Lieutenant-Governor, in Guernsey. His appointment to Gibraltar was as Commander-in-Chief and Lieutenant-Governor, the actual Governor, the Duke of Kent having been withdrawn four years earlier since his disciplinary methods had all but caused a mutiny among the garrison. Dalrymple had shown himself to be a stolid, if somewhat fussy general, but his dealings with the Spaniards had been exemplary and there could be no doubt that he knew more about the situation in Spain than any other British general. The fact remained that he had no experience of generalship in the field.

In retrospect, the appointment of Dalrymple may not have been wise but at the time it could be easily justified. Even the Opposition Press approved the appointment; the *Morning Chronicle* described him as a man of 'known enterprise, activity and experience' and added that his conduct had 'gained him the confidence of the Spanish people.'[23] That the government had its reservations is, perhaps, illustrated best by the fact that when they appointed him they laid down, for the first time, a definite objective for the expedition. 'His Majesty is pleased to direct that the attack upon the Tagus should be considered as the first object to be attended to.'[24] As long as Wellesley with 10–15,000 men only was concerned, ministers were prepared to allow him wide freedom of action. Once the force was expanded to and beyond 30,000 men and the command entrusted to a general who, if he had their confidence, was not in their confidence, the case was different. All thoughts of coastal operations against Spain were abandoned and Portugal was specified as the target.

There was one serious drawback to the nomination of Dalrymple. Since his orders must be carried down to Gibraltar, where he must hand over his command, wait for a wind which would allow him to sail westward through the straits and then northward, it was as good as certain that he would not reach the scene of action before the large reinforcements arrived from England. Ministers did not and could not know where Wellesley would go. He might go to Lisbon, to Oporto, to Vigo, Ferrol or Coruña. He might even go as far east as Santander. The further north or east he might go the sooner the reinforcements would reach him and the longer it would take Dalrymple to join. When the main reinforcements joined him the command must pass by seniority to Sir John Moore.

This Canning, as Foreign Secretary, would not allow and, despite Castlereagh's defence and championship of Moore, a majority of the cabinet agreed with Canning. Moore, the son of a fashionable Edinburgh doctor and in his early years the protégé of the Duke of Argyll, had a distinguished military career behind him. He had been outstanding as a junior officer in the American war; he had been the finest battalion commander the British army had ever had and his experience as a general was wide, varied and, by British contemporary standards, successful. Eleven years younger than Dalrymple and eight years older than Wellesley, he was, at the age of forty-seven, at the height of his powers. The army, not excluding the Duke of York as Commander-in-Chief, considered him to be their greatest living soldier. It was highly unfortunate that the appointment of commanders-in-chief for expeditions overseas was explicity a political responsibility or there can be little doubt that Moore would have been appointed.

His relationships with politicians had been less successful. Although a man of immense charm, Moore had a sharp tongue when roused and was intolerant of fools, especially of fools in high places. His last two assignments, in Sicily and Sweden, had turned out to be futile and frustrating. Both had been conceived to achieve Foreign Office rather than military ends. In addition, Moore had quarrelled, with every justification, with the Foreign Office representative in Sicily, and, although his dispatches were always couched in properly respectful terms, his private letters and conversations left no doubt that, in his opinion, Canning was a fool if not a knave. Canning, knowing this, detested Moore and took every opportunity to belittle his achievements and capability.

The cabinet would have wished to exclude Moore altogether from the Portuguese expedition. At worst they insisted that he should not be permitted to have the chief command even temporarily while awaiting the arrival of Dalrymple. They therefore instructed the Horse Guards to appoint a second-in-command who must be immediately available and senior to Moore. It was essential that he should be appointed, receive his orders and be ready to sail before Moore could be ready to sail for Portugal. The slowness of communications even within England at that time meant that the officer chosen must be either in London or the Home Counties.

In solving this problem the Horse Guards were confronted with one of the more tiresome anachronisms with which the army was encrusted. It was the immutable rule of the service that no man could be asked to serve, even for a single day, under a man whose name appeared below his in the Army list. This rule applied with particular force to general officers. Up to the rank of lieutenant-colonel promotion was a free for all, compounded of money, luck, seniority and merit. Rich officers could leapfrog their way over their poorer seniors. Gallant officers could reach even the rank of colonel by brevet. If a particularly deserving major was required for a lieutenant-colonelcy there were five or six ways of arranging it. Colonels and above rose in the service only by seniority, by what General Dundas referred to the 'usual mode of progressive advancement.' General officers were not paid unless they held a specific command or appointment so there was no objection to promoting, for example, a major-general to lieutenant-general on his merits. There was, however, the corollary that every major-general senior to the one chosen had also to be promoted in the same order on the Army list.* Only Royal Dukes could leapfrog their seniors.†

* The example may be quoted of Charles Stewart, Castlereagh's brother, who was promoted for diplomatic reasons in 1814. Sixty-two senior major-generals were promoted ahead of him, of whom only 20 had seen active service since the turn of the century and one of them not since 1756.

† The only commoner who was later an exception was the Duke of Wellington who was promoted Field-Marshal after his victory at Vitoria in 1813. He was then Lieutenant-General (local general) and was promoted over the heads of 160 seniors.

There could, therefore, be no question of promoting an officer over Moore's head. The second-in-command must come from the officers whose names appeared between those of Dalrymple, whose seniority date as lieutenant-general was 1st January 1801, and Moore, whose date was 30th October 1805.

In theory there was a wide choice. Seventy-four officers appeared in the Army list between Dalrymple and Moore. Of these, however, twelve were automatically ineligible, two of them being Royal Marines and ten belonging to one of the 'Ordnance' corps. It was unthinkable in those days for a Marine, an Artilleryman or an Engineer to hold command over cavalry or infantry. Two more, Baron Hompesch and the Count de Meuron, were foreigners, who held their rank by courtesy, having raised regiments of Germans and *emigré* Frenchmen for the British service. Lieutenant-Generals the Duke of Richmond and the Earl of Chatham were both senior cabinet ministers and it would savour of a government job if either the Lord-Lieutenant of Ireland or the Master-General of the Ordnance should be appointed to succeed the Chief Secretary for Ireland in an important command. Three more eligible officers held commands in India or the colonies. One was on the voyage back from the West Indies and another was on a special mission to Vienna. The need for speed made it impossible to secure the services of eight generals who held commands outside London in Great Britain, Ireland or the Channel Islands and other factors militated against the appointment of Lieutenant-General Oliver de Lancey, who at the turn of the century had been dismissed from his post as Barrackmaster-General for 'culpable carelessness in the accounts.' These considerations disposed of twenty-nine of the seventy-four contenders. At least fourteen more were even older than Sir Hew, one of them, James Hetherset, having been born in 1734.

The thirty-one who remained were not an inspiring collection. Only one of them had seen active service since the turn of the century and that one, Lord Hutchinson, being Governor of Stirling Castle, a Whig and of uncertain temper, was inaccessible, unacceptable and unsuitable. Four others had, apart from their

1. *Major-General the Hon. Sir Arthur Wellesley, KB*

2. *Sir Hew Dalrymple*

3. *Sir Harry Burrard*

4. *General Junot*

5. *Sir John Moore*

title of lieutenant-general, no military connection, except that they drew the half-pay of regimental officers of regiments disbanded at the end of the American War of Independence. 'The usual mode of progressive advancement' had seen to their subsequent promotion. Faced with the remainder, the Duke of York chose Sir Harry Burrard who was in London, commanding the First Guards. He was an amiable man, on terms of friendship with both Moore and the Duke. If Sir John had to be superseded, and in this the Duke had no choice, it seemed best to supersede him by a man who was at least agreeable to him.

Sir Harry Burrard was fifty-three and had been in the army since 1772. His first commission had been in the Coldstream Guards but, on the outbreak of the American war, he had exchanged into the Sixtieth Royal Americans in order to see active service. He had fought four campaigns in America with a break in 1780 when he had returned to England to inherit his uncle's seat in Parliament for Lymington, a seat he had periodically resumed until 1802. Returning to England in 1782 he had exchanged into the First Guards and, five years later, had been made Governor of Calshott Castle, a reward, presumably more for political than military services, since his rank at that time was no more than lieutenant and captain.* He fought the three years of the Flanders campaign as a regimental officer and became a major-general in 1796. His next active experience was unfortunate through no fault of his own. In 1798 he commanded a brigade in a raiding force which was landed to destroy the locks on the Bruges canal. The task was admirably performed but the weather changed, the surf rose and the force could not be re-embarked and was captured. Burrard was soon exchanged for a French general and was able to command another brigade in the abortive Helder expedition of 1799, a duty he seems to have performed with competence. Most of the intervening years he had spent in London, commanding his regiment as senior lieutenant-colonel, but in 1807 he had accompanied the Copen-

---

* Officers of the Brigade of Guards held an army rank one step above their regimental rank. Thus a lieutenant in the Guards was a captain in the army.

hagen expedition as second-in-command. In this capacity he had been called upon to do nothing of consequence but he was rewarded with a baronetcy on his return. He was, in fact, an amiable old buffer who could command a brigade provided that he was not expected to do anything too complicated. Everyone who knew him liked him but no one had a very high opinion of his mental equipment.

The cabinet had hoped that Burrard's appointment would force Moore to withdraw from the expedition to Portugal but they were disappointed. Sir John had a stormy interview with Castlereagh at which he complained that: 'Had I been an ensign, it would hardly have been possible to treat me with less ceremony. . . . I have been treated unworthily.'[25]. He was, however, too good and loyal a soldier to resign over a deliberate slight from ministers. Ministers tried again. They wrote to him telling that his complaint had been passed to the King, adding that 'had not the arrangements of the army been so far advanced as that they could not be undone without considerable detriment to His Majesty's service, there would have been every disposition on their part humbly to have advised His Majesty to relieve you from a situation in which you appear to consider yourself to have been placed without a due attention to your feelings as an officer.'[26] It was a clear invitation to resign but Moore merely replied that 'I have the most perfect reliance on His Majesty's justice, and shall never feel greater security than when my conduct, my character, and my honour are under His Majesty's protection.' 'I am', he wrote, 'about to proceed on the service on which I have been ordered, and I shall endeavour to acquit myself with the same zeal by which I have ever been actuated when employed in the service of my country.'[27]

All in all, the government had behaved with striking ineptitude. Sir Hew Dalrymple had been given command of one of the largest and finest armies that had ever been entrusted to a British general but it was entrusted to him in such a way that he felt only suspicion and resentment. His letter of service appointed him to the chief command only 'for the present' and ordered him to hand over the charge of Gibraltar to the next

66

senior officer 'during your absence.'[28] Moreover Castlereagh was tactless enough, in a private letter to him, to write: 'Permit me to recommend to your particular confidence Lieut.-Gen. Sir Arthur Wellesley. His high reputation in the service as an officer would in itself dispose you, I am persuaded, to select him for any service that required great prudence and temper, combined with much military experience. The degree, however, to which he has been for a length of time past in the closest habits of communication with His Majesty's Ministers, . . . will, I am sure, point him out to you as an officer of whom it is desirable for you, on all accounts, to make the most prominent use which the rules of the service will permit.'[29] Dalrymple was immediately alarmed that he might have been appointed to act as a whipping boy if the favoured young minister-general should fail and would be immediately returned to Gibraltar if the credit for any success could be given to Wellesley. As he wrote: 'Under the circumstances of the case, I think it can scarcely be wondered at, that I received these communications with, at least, as much surprise as satisfaction. This ebb and flow of approbation and confidence was not satisfactory; and something seemed to lurk under this most complicated arrangement, which bore, I thought, a most unpromising aspect.'[30] In fact the something that 'seemed to lurk' and made the appointment of Dalrymple temporary was almost certainly not the possible re-appointment of Wellesley to the chief command but the danger that the Duke of York might, with his royal father's support, insist on taking over the army in Portugal while Castlereagh's recommendation of Wellesley was not a deep-laid ministerial plot but the Secretary for War's misguided attempt to help a friend whom he felt he had treated shabbily.

Nor can Burrard have been happy at his position. He left no record of his feelings, but it is fair to assume from his character and subsequent actions that they were of bewilderment and an amiable desire to do his best for his country and his friend Moore, together with a vague sense of his own inadequacy. Sir Harry was not a stupid man, though he was a very cautious one, and it cannot have escaped his attention that he had been put in an invidious position. It seems probable that he only accepted the posting in the knowledge that if he did not, someone less acceptable to Moore would certainly be appointed.

Moore had been deliberately affronted by the cabinet. Short of dismissing him, a course that would have led to a public and military outcry, they had done everything they could to exclude him from the expedition. They behaved so badly to him that they brought down on their own heads a rebuke from the King. A lesser man than Moore would have resigned but that was not his way. Before leaving England he wrote to his mother 'The treatment I have received gives me no longer any uneasiness.'[31]

Wellesley, of course, had great reason for feeling aggrieved. It was a particularly unfortunate coincidence that the letter announcing his supersession should have arrived when it did, when his mind was burdened with all the chances and calculations of invading a country occupied by an enemy whose strength he had just learned to be twice the numbers he had in hand. Nevertheless, he cannot have been wholly surprised. Even before he left Cork, newspapers had been speculating about whether the Duke of York or the Earl of Chatham would be chosen to take over if the force was to be expanded. A determined realism was one of Wellesley's most prominent characteristics and he must have realised that, as a very junior lieutenant-general, he had no chance of retaining the command once the government resolved to build up his small force into a large army. As with Dalrymple, it was the manner of his supersession rather than the fact that was annoying. Moore he would gladly have served under but neither Dalrymple nor Burrard had a part of his own experience. Thirteen years before he had meditated leaving the army because 'I see the manner in which military offices are filled.'[32] Now he felt the same. To make matters worse the same dispatch told him that Lieutenant-Generals John Hope, Lord Paget and Mackenzie Fraser, all his seniors, were posted to the army. At one blow he was reduced from Commander of the Forces to the junior divisional commander.

It was a poor way to start a campaign.

References

Chapter 3. 'So Young a Lieutenant-General

1   SD xiii 291. AW to Richmond, 21 July '08
2   SD vi 89–90. AW to Gordon, 21 July '08
3   SD xiii 291. AW to Richmond, 21 July '08
4   SD vi 89. AW to Gordon, 21 July '08
5   SD xiii 291. AW to Richmond, 21 July '08
6   WD iv 39. AW to Castlereagh, 21 July '08
7   ib
8   ib
9   WD iv 42. AW to Castlereagh, 25 July '08
10 Cintra 291. Cotton to AW, 9 July '08
11 Cintra 295. Spencer to AW, 9 July '08
12 WD iv 47. AW to Castlereagh, 26 July '08
13 WD iv 44. AW to Spencer, 26 July '08
14 WD iv 48–50. Memorandum for disembarkation, 29 July '08
15 WD iv 57–58. Memorandum for the Commissary General, 1 Aug '08
16 WD iv 58–59. Proclamation to the People of Portugal, 2 Aug '08
17 SD vi 91. General Order, 31 July '08
18 WD iv 50. AW to Cotton, 30 July '08
19 WD iv 30. Castlereagh to AW, 15 July '08
20 WD iv 55. AW to Castlereagh, 1 Aug '08
21 SD vi 95. AW to Richmond, 1 Aug '08
22 Croker ii 342
23 MC 18, July '08
24 WD iv 28. Castlereagh to AW, 15 July '08
25 Moore Diary ii 242
26 Moore Diary ii 251–2. Castlereagh to Moore, 22 July '08
27 Moore Diary ii 252. Moore to Castlereagh 23 July '08
28 HD 48–49. Castlereagh to HD, 15 July '08
29 WD iv 31. Castlereagh to HD, 15 July '08
30 HD 52
31 Q: in *Carola Oman*, p. 494
32 Letter of 25 June '95, q. in Brialmont and Gleig i 22

4

'The Dash and Eagerness

GENERAL ANDROCHE JUNOT, newly created Duke of Abrantes, reigned in state in Lisbon. The palace of Queluz had been redecorated for his use and he had decked it with art treasures looted from the churches and great houses of Lisbon. His rise had been very swift. At the siege of Toulon in 1793 he had been in the ranks of the artillery and had attracted the attention of Colonel Bonaparte by his spectacular bravery. When Bonaparte became a general he took Junot, newly commissioned, as his first aide-de-camp and as Bonaparte had risen so had Junot. In 1808 he was thirty-seven and his courage was a by-word throughout the Imperial army. He had, however, little experience of independent command. Napoleon chose him for Portugal as a reward for good service as Governor of Paris during the campaign of 1806 and because he knew Lisbon, having done a short spell there as French Ambassador. He was a poor choice. In the opinion of his Chief of Staff, 'General Junot had no idea of discretion. His nickname in the army was "The Hurricane" and it was not in his nature to use his advantages with moderation. Without being proud he was vain; though good-natured he could be offensive; he was quick tempered and devoid of tact when handling people of rank and authority.'[1]

He had set out on the Portuguese campaign intent on winning a Marshal's baton and at first all had gone well. His troops, the 25,000 men of the 'Corps of Observation of the Gironde', had been received with delight by the Spaniards. Everything seemed set for a triumph until he reached Salamanca on 12th November 1807. From that day the whole campaign had gone sour on him. At Salamanca a dispatch from the Emperor had overtaken him ordering him to abandon the main road to Lisbon which ran through Coimbra and, instead, to advance on Lisbon along the line of the Tagus from Alcantara by way of Abrantes, the shortest distance from the frontier to the capital. To reach Alcantara, crossing the Pass of Perales in pitiless rain, had cost him half his horses and most of his guns. At Alcantara the Spanish division which was due to join him was not ready to move. He took from them a troop of horse artillery and all their rations and ammunition; his own powder was too wet to fire. The march from Alcantara was even worse than that over the Pass of Perales. The road along the north bank of the Tagus existed on the Emperor's map but not on the ground. Eventually he reached Lisbon on 30th November and the gates of the city were opened to him by the Chief of Police, a French *emigré*.

Not a shot was fired. As his Chief of Staff wrote, 'Junot took possession of Lisbon and of the entire kingdom without having in hand a single trooper, a single gun or a cartridge that would fire; with nothing, indeed, save the 1,500 grenadiers remaining from the four battalions of his advanced guard. Fagged out, unwashed, ghastly objects, these grenadiers no longer had even the strength to march to the beat of the drum. . . . The rest of the army dropped in over the next two days in still worse condition; some falling dead at the gates of the city.'[2] The Prince Regent of Portugal and his fleet had gone.

The Portuguese accepted the French occupation with sullen resignation. There was a riot, savagely suppressed, when the Tricolour replaced the Portuguese flag on the castle, but, in the early days Junot tried to do what he could to bring good government to the country. In this he was frustrated by his master who insisted on severity. 'You are in a conquered country and you behave as if you were in Burgundy,'[3] complained Napoleon. 'Do not seek popularity in Lisbon, or try to please the Portuguese; to do this would be to lose sight of your aim; it will embolden the people and lay up trouble for you.'[4] The Portuguese economy was already strangled by the British blockade and to complete the ruin of the country the Emperor decreed that, apart from supplying the pay and rations of the French occupying force, Portugal should pay an extraordinary tax of 100,000,000 gold francs, rather more than 50 francs for every man, woman and child of the population. It proved largely uncollectable but the attempt to collect it increased the resentment of the Portuguese people who were steadily moving towards revolt.

The May insurrection in Spain brought matters to a head. The Spanish division which had been occupying Oporto arrested the French governor and his escort and marched for Galicia leaving northern Portugal to the care of the Bishop of Oporto and his Junta. The Spanish troops south of the Tagus marched for Badajoz. In central Portugal Junot managed to disarm and imprison the Spanish division of General Caraffa, but the rest of the country burst into revolt. Two French flying columns were sent out to restore peace but they achieved nothing but bloodshed and looting. The French army in Portugal, after taking on the strength 4,000 reinforcements who had arrived before the road from Spain had been closed, was a little more than 26,000 strong. From this number had to be found garrisons for the frontier fortresses of Almeida and Elvas and for the forts of St. Julian, Cascais and Bugio which commanded the mouth of the Tagus. The ports of Peniche and Setubal had also to be manned and Lisbon, where there were 5,000 Spanish prisoners and an increasingly hostile mob, needed a strong garrison. When, during June, reports came in that the British were intending a landing, it was small wonder that Junot felt insecure.

Another cause for concern was the presence of the Russian squadron in the Tagus. With their guns trained on the town, they could have done much to keep the Lisbon mob in order. Landing parties from their 6,000 seamen and Marines could have garrisoned the castle and relieved the French of much, if not all, of their task of policing the capital. The Russians gave Junot no help at all. Admiral Siniavin contented himself with asserting that the Czar was not at war with Portugal and had never recognised the French occupation of the country. He admitted, reluctantly, that Russia was at war with Britain but he made it clear that, in his opinion, this was a misfortune. It never crossed his mind to take his ships to sea and to face Admiral Cotton's squadron which his own greatly outnumbered. He did nothing, in fact, except to demand rations at a time when Junot was being increasingly hard put to it to find food for his own men.

From Spain and France Junot heard nothing.

*   *   *

Early on the morning of 1st August the riflemen of General Fane's brigade started landing from their transports at the mouth of the Mondego. It was a difficult and dangerous operation. They had, first, to be transferred to schooners and local coasting craft or to ship's boats as there was a bar across the river mouth which would not allow of boats drawing more than eleven feet. Over the bar there was a considerable surf. At first there was a gentle inshore breeze but later although 'the surface of the sea was as smooth as glass, a heavy ground swell set in from the Atlantic, causing the ships to roll so heavily that it was a matter of great difficulty to get on board or leave them.'[5] There were no French for many miles, a fact that was regarded as a great blessing in view of the difficulty of landing. 'Had we been opposed from the land', wrote a staff officer, 'I am positive we should never have effected it, so great is the surf both on the coast and on the bar.'[6]

The first troops ashore had an almost overwhelming reception from the inhabitants. A company commander of the Ninety-Fifth recalled that 'whilst we were drawing up our men near the landing place, and waiting for further orders, we were beset with a host of padres, friars, monks of all ages, each carrying a huge umbrella of the most gaudy colour imaginable; intended, no doubt, to protect their complexions, which vied with those of chimney sweeps. These gentry welcomed us with *vivas*, and protested that, with our assistance, every Frenchman in Portugal should be speedily annihilated. Our visitors were not confined to the male sex; for some olive beauties, with sparkling eyes and jet black hair, were induced to take a peep at us; and before we parted, some of the more favoured of us were presented with flowers and fruit from the hands of these damsels.'[7]

As soon as the battalions were formed they marched off about five miles to the south where they encamped around the little village of Lavos, but landing the army was a long business and it was not until the evening of 5th August that all were ashore. Getting the sparse cavalry to the beach was a particularly difficult business. 'We were directed to stand upright in the boats, with bridle in hand, and prepared, in case of any accident, to spring into the saddle; a judicious precaution which proved in two or three instances eminently useful. One punt capsized upon the surf, but no lives were lost, because the horses, sometimes swimming, sometimes wading, carried their riders ashore.'[8] Just

74

as the last of Wellesley's troops from Ireland were ashore, another convoy reached Mondego Bay bearing General Spencer and his division. It was not until the evening of 8th August that the whole force, 13,500 strong, was ashore.

In the meantime there was much to be attended to. The army had to be split up into six brigades and half a battery of field artillery attached to each. The organisation of the Commissariat demanded Wellesley's constant and detailed attention. 'That department is very incompetent', he wrote to Castlereagh. 'The existence of the army depends upon it, and yet the people who manage it are incapable of managing anything out of a counting house.'[9] Nor was the Commissariat side of the artillery, which was, of course, quite separate from that of the cavalry and infantry, any better. He had fully to agree with Colonel Robe, commanding the artillery that the establishment of the civil department for that arm 'being only one clerk of stores, who is also Paymaster, and five conductors of stores, two of whom have never yet joined', was quite insufficient. He was, however, unable to do anything about it, or even to authorise Colonel Robe to have a staff officer, since the Board of Ordnance had not seen fit to depute to him the necessary powers.[10]

As far as producing troops went, Portuguese help turned out to be largely an illusion. Wellesley had hoped to have the support of 5,000 Portuguese and landed sufficient muskets to arm them but on 7th August he met their general, Bernadino Freire, at Montemor-o-Velho and found him an impossible colleague. The Portuguese was most reluctant to serve under a British officer, insisted that the army should march on Santarem, and declared that his troops could not advance in any direction unless they were provisioned by the British. Both these last two stipulations were, as Freire probably realised, impossible for Wellesley to agree. He was inevitably tied to the coast road since he could only feed his troops from the victualling ships with the fleet, and these could not provide for 5,000 Portuguese for any length of time. In the end a compromise was reached. Freire took the bulk of his troops away eastward leaving with Wellesley some two hundred horsemen and 1,400 light infantry, under an eccentric British officer in the Portuguese service, Colonel Nicholas Trant. It was not a great loss. From what he had seen of the Portuguese troops he had formed no high opinion of them: 'they cannot in any respect be deemed an efficient force,'[11] he had written. As for Freire and his colleagues: 'The fact is, they are afraid of the French, they are not capable of making any arrangement to feed their troops; and they are not a little afraid of them.'*[12]

On the supply side the situation was somewhat better. 500 mules and 300 bullock carts were acquired, beside enough troop horses to bring the mounted strength of the Twentieth Dragoons up to 240. Although, with the guns which Spencer had brought from Gibraltar, five batteries were available, it was only possible to find horses for three of them, one of nine pounders and two of six pounders, the situation being made worse by the need to put two horses 'in addition to the usual number in each carriage, on account of the heaviness and badness of the roads, the heat of the weather and the low condition' of the horses sent from Ireland.[13] There was no help to be got in this matter from Portuguese horses as although 'good of their kind,' they were 'but small, and not of sufficient weight for our carriages.'[14]

On 10th August all was ready and the army set off for the south. 'The soldiers had each of them sixty rounds of musket ammunition; besides this quantity there were ninety mules attached to the reserve of the artillery to carry musket ammunition, each mule with 2,000 rounds; and there were 500,000 rounds on carts. The army marched with seventeen days' bread, viz. four days' bread on the men's backs, three days' bread on mules, and ten on carts; there were besides five days' salt meat, and ten days' spirits.'[15] A contract had been made with a Portuguese merchant for fresh meat to accompany the army on the hoof, but for the first few days of the march the contractor was not able to keep three days' fresh meat with the army as he had engaged to do. On the first day the march was a short one, only twelve miles, to Lugar but, for the men who had been

* Bernardino Freire was murdered by a mob which accused
  him of cowardice in the following year.

cooped up in transports for many weeks it was hard, especially as they 'were up to their knees in sand and suffering dreadfully from thirst.[16] There were many stragglers. The second day's march took them to Leiria where the army saw its first signs of the French occupation. 'The town bore every mark of recent depredation, plunder and excess of all kinds. The walls of a convent, into which I went with some other officers, were covered with blood and brains in many places. . . . As yet, the only specimens of the French army we had seen, were five Swiss deserters, from their infantry, clothed in scarlet, and remarkably fine looking men.'[17]

The picture of the French strength in Portugal was slowly becoming clearer, although all the sources gave too low a total. Whereas Junot's actual strength was 26,000, Wellesley wrote on 8th August that 'the enemy's force at present in Portugal consists, as far as I am able to form an opinion, of from 16,000 to 18,000 men.'[18] From Leiria, on 11th August, he gave a more detailed breakdown. 'About 5,000 or 6,000 occupy Lisbon, Forts St. Julian and Cascais and the other works erected for the defence of the Tagus and of the Bay of Lisbon; 800 in Peniche, 600 in Almeida, 600 in Elvas and, it is said, 1,600 in Setubal; of the disposable force about 4,000 are at Alcobaça, about sixteen miles from hence, under Generals Laborde and Thomières, and the remainder, under Generals Junot and Loison, are in the neighbourhood of Santarem.'[19] It was not, as far as troops actually available went, inaccurate except that Delaborde's force at Alcobaça was over 5,000 strong with five guns; Loison did not reach Santarem from Elvas, in which direction he had been making a *chevauchée* in an attempt to overawe Alemtejo, until two days later, and Junot, who had learned of the British landing on 2nd August, was still in Lisbon, making arrangements for the capital to be garrisoned. He believed that the situation there was so explosive that the force available from the garrison for field operations was less than 3,000 men with ten guns.

It was Wellesley's intention to march directly on Lisbon, keeping close to the shore to enable him not only to feed his troops from the victualling ships but, more important still, to be able to cover the disembarkation of the brigades of Acland and Anstruther, which he expected to arrive at any time, and which he believed he required in order to be certain of defeating Junot in an attacking battle. He left at Figueira da Foz a letter for Sir Harry Burrard, recommending him to land Moore's corps at that port and, as soon as transport could be found for it, to march with all speed for Santarem, where it would be excellently placed to cut off the French from both Elvas and Almeida. While urging Burrard to march to Santarem, Wellesley did not conceal from him that the large reinforcement would have difficulties in supplying itself with food and transport. 'You will find the people of this country well disposed to assist you with everything in their power, but they have very little in their power, and they have been terribly plundered by the French. . . . In the present season of the year, you cannot depend upon the country for bread. Portugal never fed itself during more than seven months out of twelve. The common consumption of the country is Indian corn; and the little which there is in the country cannot be ground at this season of the year, as the mills are generally turned by water, and there is now no water in the mill streams; you must therefore depend upon your transports for bread. Wine and beef you will get in the country. I have ordered 150 draught mules from Oporto, . . . and you will of course take them. As for mules for carriages, I am afraid you will get none; for I believe my corps has swept the country, very handsomely, of this animal. You must therefore depend for the carriage of your bread upon the carts of the country drawn by bullocks, . . . but I do not believe that any power you could exert over them . . . would induce the owners of the carts to go from their homes a greater distance than to the nearest place where you could get carts to relieve them.'[20]

Having left some heavy baggage and all its tents in Leiria the army pushed forward slowly on 13th August, having waited there for twenty-four hours to enable stragglers and supplies to catch up. They hoped to meet the enemy that day but Delaborde, who had planned to stand by the old abbey of Batalha, where the Portuguese under John of Gaunt's son-in-law had broken the Spanish invaders in 1385, failed to find a sufficiently strong position and fell back before them. It was not until the evening of the 15th that the first shots were fired.

On that day, while headquarters were moving into Caldas, the advanced guard, four companies of Riflemen and a patrol of Light Dragoons bumped the enemy. Approaching the old castle of Obidos where it dominates the road as it crosses a ridge, they came under fire from a windmill and a group of cottages. The Riflemen were over-eager and, 'one of the skirmishers jumping up, rushed forward, crying "Over, boys, – Over, Over!" when instantly the whole line responded to the cry, "Over, Over, Over!" They ran along the grass like wildfire, and dashed at the rise, fixing their sword bayonets as they ran. The French light-bobs could not stand the sight, and, getting possession of the ground, we were soon inside the buildings.'[21] So far no harm had been done but, as a young Rifle officer admitted in his diary, 'being rather too elevated with this, our first collision with the foe, we dashed along the plain after them like young soldiers.'[22] Three companies of the Sixtieth and one of the Ninety-Fifth chased the *voltigeurs* for three miles until they approached the main French position. Delaborde sent out a strong force of infantry and cavalry to cut them off and for a few minutes their situation was grave. Fortunately, General Spencer was on the Obidos ridge and saw their danger. He ordered up a brigade of infantry which brought them off with only thirty-one casualties, including two officers. Although irritated by the lack of discipline which the men had shown, Wellesley was not wholly displeased. He reported to London: 'The affair of the advanced posts yesterday was unpleasant, because it was quite useless; and was occasioned, contrary to orders, solely by the imprudence of the officer, and the dash and eagerness of the men: they behaved remarkably well, and did some execution with their rifles.'[23]

At Caldas the army again halted for twenty-four hours to allow the bullock carts with supplies to keep up with the advance. Beef and wine were available from the Portuguese contractor and only bread and ammunition had to come from the fleet but Wellesley was taking no chances and he was determined that no one would be able to accuse him of breaking his undertaking not to 'hurry the operations, . . . in order that I may acquire the credit of the success.' (*see p.* 59) His information was that Delaborde had about 4,000 men in his immediate front and that Loison was at Rio Maior with about 5,000 and marching to join Junot with whatever could be spared from the Lisbon garrison. This was correct except that both Delaborde and Loison were about 1,000 men stronger than reports showed and that Loison was at Alcoentre, about eight miles further south, and nearer Lisbon, than Rio Maior. There was no news of his own reinforcements, the brigades of Acland and Anstruther. On the whole he had reason to be satisfied and he wrote to Castlereagh: 'We are going on as well as possible; the army in high order and in great spirits. We make long marches, to which they are becoming accustomed; and I make no doubt they will be equal to anything when we shall reach Lisbon. I have every hope of success.'[24]

Delaborde, meanwhile, kept his troops around Roliça, a village on the slopes of a small conical hill rising from the surrounding plain. He had no intention of fighting a battle – he knew that his numbers were too small to enable him to bring the British to a halt. He meant nothing more than to delay Wellesley by making him deploy. By making a bold stand on a reasonably strong position he knew that he could make his opponent waste at least half a day while he sent forces round the French flanks. He knew that such flanking attacks would take place but since his cavalry was twice as strong as Wellesley's he knew that, before the flanking attacks could be launched, he could draw off his infantry and guns in safety.

Wellesley agreed exactly with Delaborde on the way in which the fighting should go. Nothing was further from his mind than a series of frontal assaults on positions of Delaborde's choosing. Such attacks would cause unnecessary losses, use up valuable ammunition and, since he had determined not to hurry, would gain nothing. Therefore, at 7 o'clock on the morning of 17th

6. *Vimeiro. The Highlanders turning captured guns on the French*

7.   *Vimeiro. The attack on the 43rd*

8.   *Vimeiro. Sir Arthur Wellesley directs the battle*

August the army moved forward in three columns to drive Delaborde back. On the right marched most of the Portuguese infantry with a weak squadron of their cavalry; in the centre four British brigades with most of the cavalry and two batteries; while on the left two brigades supported by a battery of six pounders, three companies of Rifles and forty horsemen set off to turn the French right. The lefthand column had the additional duty 'to watch the motions of General Loison on the enemy's right, who, I had heard, had moved from Rio Maior towards Alcoentre last night.'

That morning the plans of both sides worked perfectly. There was a sharp engagement of light troops along the front of the French position while behind them the brigades of the British centre advanced slowly in beautiful order, their drill exciting the admiration of the enemy. As soon as the flanking columns began to press in on the French, Delaborde gave the order to withdraw and, covered by their cavalry, the French infantry marched to the rear, briskly but in good order, and took up another position rather more than a mile further back.

The new position, near the village of Columbeira, was a much more formidable obstacle. It was a sharp line of hills broken at intervals with dry watercourses. Even had Wellesley been in a hurry, it would have been a most dangerous place on which to deliver a frontal attack. As one British officer wrote, 'the hill was as steep as that at Malvern, and covered with loose pebbles, having only a few stunted shrubs here and there to give security to the footing.'[25] Although it was now mid-day, orders were given for the morning's manœuvre to be repeated. The Portuguese again swung out to the right while on the left General Ferguson and his two brigades struck out south-east to circumvent the steepest of the hills facing them. Meanwhile the British artillery unlimbered on the southern slopes of Roliça hill and started pounding the crest of the French position while the Riflemen went forward to skirmish amongst the scant cover at the foot of the escarpment. The summer sun was at its height. 'Neither before or since', wrote a captain, 'do I remember to have felt more intense and suffocating heat than we experienced in climbing to the attack; every mouthful of air was such as is inhaled when looking into an oven.'[26]

In an attempt to reduce the chances of the French being able to break contact with the ease with which they had done so during the morning, Wellesley brought forward the bulk of the centre column intending to launch one battalion with another in support up each of the four dry watercourses which intersected the front of the French position. It was his intention, clearly understood in three of the four cases, that no attempt should be made to attack until the French were engaged on their flanks by Ferguson and the Portuguese. Unfortunately, Ferguson was delayed by losing his track in the difficult country he had to traverse and the Portuguese on the right never came into action at all. In the meantime, Lieut.-Col. the Hon. George Lake, son of Wellesley's former colleague in India, General Lord Lake, who was either hot-headed or had misunderstood his orders, led the Twenty-Ninth straight up the gully allotted to him. The battalion needed no urging. 'Though obliged at times to climb on hands and feet, nothing could restrain their impetuosity.'[27] Under a heavy fire from front and flanks the Worcesters, led by their colonel, conspicuous on his charger, reached the crest, to be greeted by a rabble of Swiss who wished to desert. Their first need was to form line, for all order had been lost in their scramble up the watercourse, but before they could do so they were charged in flank and rear by a full French battalion. Lake was killed, four officers captured together with many men and the remainder fell back down the steep slope, only to rally and attack once more in company with their supporting battalion, the Ninth, whose colonel was mortally wounded. Three times this small battered force, struggled to the crest and the third time they stayed there, the Twenty-Ninth having lost 190 and the Ninth 72 officers and men.

With Ferguson's column still not making its appearance, Wellesley was forced to do what he could to extricate the two impetuous battalions and ordered the attacks up the other gullies to go forward. In each case there was a sharp struggle at the top but, before heavy casualties could be suffered, Ferguson's men appeared on Delaborde's right and the Frenchman gave orders for instant retreat. The French pulled back most skilfully, pairs of battalions covering each other as they went with the cavalry constantly threatening the pursuers, but with the British infantry actually in contact the retreat was not the field day manœuvre that it had been in the morning. Two miles behind the position the road runs through a defile near the village of Zambugeira, and while the French were delayed passing through, they had to abandon three guns and some prisoners. From then on for some miles their retreat was something of a rout until Delaborde halted and re-formed them at Montechique. Wellesley, with his dearth of cavalry, did not press the pursuit.

The British losses at Roliça were 474, including 28 officers. Two battalion commanders died and more than eighty officers and men fell into French hands. The French losses were heavier, more than 600 killed and wounded, Delaborde himself being among the latter. To the extent that they had driven the French from a strong position, taken three guns and inflicted more casualties than they had suffered, the British could claim a victory but the whole battle was quite unnecessary. Had it not been for Colonel Lake's misunderstanding or impetuosity, none of the casualties need have occurred. The worst part of it was that, to those who did not know the detailed story of the battle, it gave the impression that Wellesley, with a series of unco-ordinated frontal attacks, had attempted to batter his way through a strong position. Nothing in his despatch contradicted this impression. There was no word of criticism for the impetuous Lake, only a lament for his loss and a generous mention that he 'distinguished himself on this occasion'.[28] Others were not so generous. Moore, a few weeks later, found that the French view of Roliça was that 'our soldiers were brave, but that our generals showed little conduct or experience.'[29] To those in England, both in the army and outside it, who regarded Wellesley as a political appointee with a bubble reputation gained for easy victories in India, an imputation of rashness to Wellesley was neither unexpected nor unwelcome.

Two important pieces of news reached headquarters next day.

Portuguese sources reported that Delaborde and Loison had joined forces at Torres Vedras and that they expected to be joined by Junot with the troops from Lisbon. This was false. While Roliça was being fought Junot and Loison had met at Cercal, only ten miles from Wellesley's left. There, during the night, they heard that Delaborde had fallen back to Montechique and decided to march south to join him. This involved a trying march over the western slopes of Monte Junta and it was not until late on 19th August that the whole French field force, rather more than 13,000 men with 23 guns was concentrated at Torres Vedras. The other report was true and more immediately significant. At 9 o'clock on the morning of 18th August, Wellesley received a letter from Brigadier-General Anstruther reporting that he, with his own brigade and parts of Acland's, had reached Mondego Bay where he had found the letter of instructions which Wellesley had left for Acland, as senior brigadier. Acting on these orders Anstruther had sailed to the south and had arrived, with his transports, off Peniche where he was waiting for further orders in company with the victualling ships.

No news could be more welcome to Wellesley. He had been reluctant to drive straight on Lisbon in the face of the concentrated French army before the arrival of the 4,000 men in these two brigades. Now that at least 2,500 of them were available the way was clear. He wrote to London: 'As soon as Anstruther is landed I shall be able to give you a good account of the French army; but I am afraid that I shall not gain a complete victory; that is I shall not entirely destroy them for want of cavalry.'[30]

He wrote immediately to Anstruther telling him to land to the south of Peniche, which was held by the French, and set the army marching westward to cover the disembarkation. That night he reached Lourinha and, on the following day, he personally reconnoitred and approved the beach at Maceira Bay as a landing place.

References

Chapter 4. '*The Dash and Eagerness of the Men*'

1 Thiebault ii 193
2 Thiebault ii 199
3 LIN i 136. N to Junot, 7 Jan '08
4 NC xvi 13416. N to Junot, 23 Dec '07
5 PS i 4. Wilkie
6 Warre 21
7 Leach 42
8 Hussar i 248
9 WD iv 72–73. AW to Castlereagh, 8 Aug '08
10 WD iv 71. AW to Robe, 8 Aug '08
11 WD iv 42. AW to Castlereagh, 25 July '08
12 WD iv 96. AW to Castlereagh, 16 Aug '08
13 Cintra 50. Evidence of AW
14 Duncan ii 198. Robe to Macleod, 7 Aug '08
15 Cintra 11. Evidence of AW
16 Journal of a Soldier 47
17 Leach 44
18 WD iv 66. AW to HB, 8 Aug '08
19 WD iv 82. AW to Gordon, 11 Aug '08
20 WD iv 84–85. AW to HB, 11 Aug '08
21 Harris 37
22 Cox Journal, q. in Verner i 145
23 WD iv 95. AW to Castlereagh, 16 Aug '08
24 ib
25 PS i 9. Wilkie
26 Leach 22
27 Warre 25
28 WD iv 98. AW to Castlereagh, 17 Aug '08
29 Moore Diary ii 267
30 WD iv 103. AW to Castlereagh, 18 Aug '08

'I decided that the Army

O<small>N</small> 15th July Sir Harry Burrard was told that 'it was intended to employ me as second-in-command to a force of 30,000 men, with directions to wait upon Lord Castlereagh, the Secretary of State, without loss of time; I did so, and found that the destination of the force was Portugal.'[1] That day the corps from Sweden anchored in the Downs and Moore reached London on the 16th. Thus, by a short margin, ministers had succeeded in having a second-in-command appointed before Moore returned.

It was not until 21st July that Burrard received his formal letter of service from the Horse Guards and, two days later, his final briefing from Castlereagh. He at once set off to Portsmouth where he took over the command from Moore. Even then the wind was south-westerly and the fleet could not hope to leave Portsmouth. On the 27th the wind veered east. Burrard and Moore embarked in H.M.S. *Audacious* and the fleet set sail. Within a few hours the wind swung back to south-west and they had to anchor off St. Helens for almost four days. While they waited Burrard received a letter from Castlereagh who had received Wellesley's dispatch from Coruña of the 21st. The Secretary of State reported that Wellesley had moved to Oporto,

that the Galicians were anxious that the British army should
go to Portugal and that the French strength in Portugal 'was
supposed to amount to 15,000, 12,000 of which were assembled
in Lisbon.' He strongly suggested that Burrard 'or some confidential officer' should go to Oporto 'in a light vessel' to discover
what Wellesley had decided to do. As an afterthought ('it may
be worth mentioning') he added that Admiral Cotton had
reported that his Marines had occupied the fort at Figueira
da Foz.

On 31st July, the day on which Wellesley heard of his supersession, the vast convoy finally set out from St. Helens. There
were, apart from the naval escort, 181 ships, carrying 14,218 all
ranks and 1,519 horses. The weather continued bad. Sir Harry
wrote that 'in the Channel the fleet was baffled by strong contrary winds, but by the almost unexampled exertions of Captain
Gosselin, the senior naval officer, we were enabled to keep the
sea, sending back into port a few crippled ships.'[2] It was, perhaps,
because of the heavy weather, that Sir Harry did not feel inclined
to exchange the comparative comfort of the *Audacious* for a
'light vessel' and sail ahead of his troops to Oporto, as Castlereagh had suggested.

It was not until 16th August, the day after the affair at Obidos, that the convoy reached Cape Finisterre. There they met, according to Sir John Moore, 'a frigate, by which we were informed that Sir Arthur Wellesley had landed with his troops in the Mondego river.'[3] Burrard, in his narrative of the campaign, makes no mention of this frigate, merely saying that, 'on the 16th of August, as we neared Cape Finisterre, I shifted to the *Brazen* sloop, . . . and running ahead of the fleet, we proceeded to Oporto, where we arrived on the 17th, and learnt that Sir Arthur Wellesley had landed at Mondego with the troops from Ireland, reinforced by General Spencer, and the corps under his command. Leaving directions for Sir John Moore to follow, I arrived off the Mondego on the 18th.'[4]

It seems that Sir Harry was less than frank when he gave this account of his actions. Moore, who had no reason for not writing the truth, wrote in his journal on 19th August that Burrard knew that Wellesley had landed at Mondego Bay before he left the convoy. There was thus no valid reason for Burrard to put into Oporto to learn what Wellesley had done. His obvious course of action was to go straight to the Mondego and find out from Wellesley himself. Moreover, Burrard glosses over the orders he had left with Moore. Moore says unambiguously: 'He directed me to lie off Vigo until I heard from him.'[5] As the wind was then 'blowing fresh from the north-east'[6] it would have been impossible for a ship from Oporto to reach Vigo and the fact that Moore's corps came on the scene as early as it did was due to Sir John's decision on the following day to sail down on his own initiative. He reached Mondego Bay, the wind having dropped almost to nothing, on the evening of the 20th 'but very few of the convoy got in that night or the following day, owing to calms and light winds.'[7]

Inevitably as he sailed down the west coast of Portugal, Sir Harry thought of the task ahead of him. Being a modest man, he did not think of himself as a Great Commander, but at least he had some experience of European war. He had served for three years in Flanders, for a campaign in North Holland and another in Denmark. In his youth he had seen four campaigns as an officer of light troops in broken country, so that he could feel, with confidence that he was a reliable all-rounder. He thought, too, of Wellesley, whom he had come to supersede. He knew Sir Arthur – he had known him in Denmark and in London. A withdrawn young general of thirty-nine – not a convivial man – no small talk – very formal and reserved in the presence of his seniors. His brother, that arrogant Lord Wellesley, was the man who had stirred up all that trouble when he was Governor-General in India. Sir Arthur had been out in India and neither the Board nor the servants of the East India company had been backward in suggesting that his brother had gone out of his way to create opportunities for the general to distinguish himself. In any case what could such a young general know of real soldiering? He had been too young for the American war. As a young officer he had frittered away his time as an aide-de-camp at Viceregal Lodge in Dublin when he should have been with his regiment. They said that he had done quite well in Flanders, as a battalion commander of a line regiment. He had been well spoken of for his quick thinking at Boxtel, but that was a mere skirmish, like his other European engagement – routing some inexperienced Danes on the Copenhagen expedition. It was these and his political connections which had persuaded Castlereagh, another Anglo-Irishman, to consult him about military matters and to put him in charge of the force going to the Peninsula. There were, of course, two victories in India. They had both been rash to the point of madness. Finding himself faced with vastly superior numbers, he had, on both occasions, attacked at once – and won. That might do when opposed to a parcel of blacks but it would never answer against the French, who had defeated every Continental army and had forced the British into a series of humiliating evacuations. Sir Arthur's rashness must be kept firmly in check.

The *Brazen* reached Mondego Bay on 18th August. There he found H.M.S. *Donegal* a ship of the line whose captain, Captain Malcolm, gave him three letters from Wellesley, the last of them written a week before. Of the army there was no sign save for two batteries of guns left near the beach under a slight guard, there having been no draught animals to pull them. The army had marched off southward ten days earlier. 'Some rumours had reached Captain Malcolm that day that an engagement had taken place, and as the intelligence ought to have reached him regularly, he seemed uneasy.'[8]

Sir Harry was very uneasy. He had not anticipated that Wellesley, for all his rashness, would have marched off towards Lisbon without waiting for his reinforcements and, indeed, for Sir Harry. Nor did Wellesley's letters ease his mind. Despite Sir Arthur's opinion that 'no reliance could be placed on the resources of the country', he had proposed that 'the corps of Sir John Moore should march upon Santarem on the Tagus, and there take up a position to stop the enemy should he attempt that route. . . . This disposition', Sir Harry would 'have wished to adopt at an earlier period, if I had considered Sir John Moore's division sufficiently strong to check the French army, and the intention of its chief been to force his way to Almeida. . . . The danger of pushing a corps to Santarem, much inferior in my opinion to what the enemy could have brought against it, would have made me decline that operation. By this I mean, that our division at Santarem must have been at all times inferior to the French, if they chose to push that way, and the division on the coast would have also been inferior, though in a lesser degree (according to my calculations) as they approached Lisbon, and that want of co-operation might have been equally felt by both, more especially if the sea column, made no considerable halt. On all these considerations I rather put this operation out of my mind at that time.'[9]

Poor Sir Harry was now taking counsel of his fears on a grand scale. His latest information of the French strength in Portugal, from Wellesley's letter of 8th August, was that Junot had between 16,000 and 18,000 men and that many of these (*see p.* 77) were engaged in garrison duty, some of them on the Spanish frontier. Wellesley, he knew, had 13,500 men and since Malcolm would have told him that Acland had sailed south from Mondego Bay, it would be reasonable to suppose that he now had 17,000. Moore had 14,000 and yet he regarded a battle

90

between either of these corps and Junot's disposable force as an unjustifiable risk. Without sending further orders to Moore, he put to sea again and headed south to find Wellesley and stop him doing something rash.

As Sir Harry sailed on from Figueira towards Maçeira Bay on 18th August the actual position of the troops on both sides was as follows. Wellesley, with 13,000 men and 18 guns was marching on Lourinha, which he reached that afternoon. A further 2,500 men under Brigadier-General Acland, the first instalment of the two brigades from eastern England, were sailing in company with the army's supply ships from a position off Peniche to Maçeira Bay. The remaining 1,500 men of the brigades, under Brigadier-General Anstruther, were some twenty-four hours sailing behind them. Another day's sail to the north was H.M.S. *Brazen*, carrying Sir Harry Burrard, accompanied by his senior staff officers and his aides-de-camp. Sir John Moore and the enormous convoy carrying 14,000 men were waiting, three hundred miles to the north of Maçeira, for further orders from Sir Harry. The winds, which had been light for some days, were falling steadily and none of the seaborne troops could move with any speed. Unknown to any of these troops and their generals, Sir Hew Dalrymple was a day's sailing south of the mouth of the Tagus, making the best speed he could in the frigate *Phoebe*.

On the French side, Delaborde, with 3,500 fit men and three guns surviving from Roliça, was at Montechique, some twenty-five miles from Wellesley's staging point that night at Lourinha. Ten miles to the east of him was the detachment Junot had made from the garrison of Lisbon, some 3,000 men with ten guns, which was moving up to Torres Vedras by the road from Vila Franca. Junot, himself, had ridden on ahead of them and had joined Loison who, with his column of 6,500 men and ten guns, was at Torres Vedras, twelve miles from Wellesley. The only reserves on which Junot could draw were the 6,500 men he had left in garrison at Lisbon. A few thousand more troops were scattered about Portugal in garrisons but, apart from 800 Germans at Santarem, none of these could be called up to the main army in less than ten days. Six unfortunate companies of Swiss were guarding the fortress of Peniche on the coast and were irretrievably cut off by Wellesley's march to Louriha. Thus, as soon as Acland and Anstruther had been landed, Wellesley would comfortably outnumber Junot and, even had Wellesley been defeated, Moore could bring equal numbers to avenge him.

All this, however, was obscure to Burrard as he sailed, with a light breeze towards Maçeiro Bay. On 19th August, off São Martinho do Porto, 'we spoke a dispatch boat with two English soldiers and a marine, who were returning from St. Martins to the Burlings; from them we learned that a sharp action had taken place on the 17th, at or near Obidos, and that a great many men were killed on both sides, that we had suffered much, but that the enemy had retreated. The man gave me so many proofs of having been present at what he said he had seen, that I could have no doubt, and I therefore became extremely anxious that some part, or all, of Sir John Moore's corps should land at Mondego, and either support Sir Arthur Wellesley, if his division should be obliged to fall back, or to assist it to advance, if a superior force had stopped it on some position which he might have chosen, thinking it practical in such case that Sir John Moore, by great exertion, might be enabled to form a junction with Sir Arthur Wellesley, with all or some part of his division. It was evident, from the intelligence of these men, that Peniche was not in our possession, and I knew of no certainty, or even probability of a landing elsewhere to the south of it. Indeed, we had always been given to understand that there was no safe landing south of Peniche.'[10]

Thus, from a garbled account of the battle of Roliça, given him by two private soldiers and a marine, Sir Harry's fears were raised to an even higher pitch. Sir Arthur, he believed, had gone bald-headed at a small French division and had won a minor success at heavy cost. It confirmed all his fears of Wellesley's rashness. He immediately sent a staff officer in the dispatch boat with a letter to Moore, enclosing copies of Wellesley's recent letters and saying in his covering letter, 'I was in hopes of an early interview with Sir A. Wellesley, . . . but I am sorry to say that calms and contrary winds have baffled all our exertions and I begin to be apprehensive that, should he meet with a superior force, he will have nothing to fall back upon; and as I find that he means to go directly on to the attack of Junot at Lisbon, there is no time to be lost . . . I think you cannot do better than to land with all expedition, procuring as many mules and bullock carts as you can, and proceeding to Leiria.'[11] It is clear that Sir Harry expected nothing but disaster from Sir Arthur's precipitate proceedings.

Having taken this wholly negative action, Sir Harry sailed again with a light wind and on the afternoon of the 20th arrived off Maçeira Bay where there was a great concentration of shipping. Anstruther's brigade was ashore, part of Acland's was in process of landing, and the remainder was coming up to the beach 'but almost becalmed'.

Whatever fears Sir Harry may have had for his safety, Sir Arthur was in high spirits. From Lourinha on the 18th he had issued a General Order expressing himself 'perfectly satisfied with the conduct of the troops in the action of yesterday, particularly with the gallantry displayed by the 5th, 9th, 29th, 60th and 95th, to whose lot it principally fell to engage the enemy. From the specimen afforded yesterday of their behaviour in action, the lieutenant-general feels confident that the troops will distinguish themselves whenever the enemy may give them another occasion.'[12] The following day he marched to a position with his right near the sea and his left at the village of Vimeiro. The troops were drawn up on a strong ridge facing south with one flank protected by the sea and the other by a sharp cleft in the ridge through which flowed the river Maçeira.* A mile behind his right flank Anstruther and Acland landed their brigades. The surf here was even more dangerous than at Mondego Bay, 'the boats', wrote the naval officer in charge, 'were almost constantly filled in going in by the surf'[13] but few if any lives were lost,

---

* The river is actually called the Alcabrichel, but all British accounts refer to it as the Maçeira from the village near its mouth.

although the sailors were apprehensive that any day the strong westerly winds from the Atlantic would start blowing and make landing impossible. Dr. Neale, who landed with Anstruther, wrote that 'the spot where we landed is a sandy beach at the foot of an almost perpendicular cliff. On the summit are the ruins of an old quadrangular fort, to which we were conducted by a narrow winding path, very steep and difficult of ascent. Behind lies a heath where we took up our abode for the night.'[14] By the 20th Anstruther's brigade had taken up its place in the line and Acland's was beginning to move up. The army was 16,700 strong, apart from 2,000 Portuguese, a force adequate to deal with any number that Junot could be expected to bring against it.

The supply situation was satisfactory. Fresh meat was plentiful and, even allowing for the reinforcements who had arrived carrying with them four days' bread, the army had in camp supplies for ten days and the means of moving them.

Wellesley knew that Junot had concentrated his field force at Torres Vedras and rightly suspected that it was the French general's intention to attack him. This was a prospect which did not distress him in the slightest. His own intention was to attack as soon as Acland was ashore and ready. In the meanwhile his only concern was the activities of the French cavalry who far outnumbered his own 240 dragoons even when augmented by about the same number of Portuguese horsemen. 'Their cavalry was very active throughout the days of the 19th and 20th, they covered the country, patrolled frequently up to our position, and on the 20th one patrol was pushed into the rear of our right, as far as the landing place.'[15] The French cavalry did no harm, however, and even failed to report to Junot that substantial reinforcements were landing.

It was not Wellesley's intention to advance against Junot in the strong position of Torres Vedras. He had no detailed map of the country in which he was operating, the Board of Ordnance having been unable to issue him with any except for the district immediately surrounding Lisbon. Nor was he able, thanks to the French cavalry, to patrol forward, but his information was

94

that if he stuck to the coast road he could turn the Torres Vedras position and lay his army, with its advanced guard at Mafra, on the flank of Junot and in a position to reach Lisbon before the French. About midday he issued his orders. 'The army will march at half-past four o'clock tomorrow morning. Half a pint of wine per man, and one day's meat for tomorrow, to be issued at four this evening to all the troops excepting Brigadier-General Anstruther's brigade, which will receive one pint of wine per man.'[16] Soon after he had issued these orders a message reached him that the *Brazen* with Sir Harry Burrard on board had anchored in Maçeira Bay. Taking Colonel Henry Torrens, his Military Secretary, and Captain Lord Burghersh, his aide-de-camp, he rode down to the beach, and in a ship's boat was rowed the mile and a half out to where the *Brazen* lay.

On arrival he went into conference with Sir Harry, who was accompanied by Brigadier-General Henry Clinton, his Adjutant-General, and Colonel George Murray, Quartermaster-General. Wellesley first gave him a short description of the campaign so far and then, according to Burrard, 'told me most fully what the difficulties were I should have to encounter; he mentioned his want of cavalry, and the inefficiency of the artillery horse, and that the enemy were strong in the former; that their cavalry had already come very near them, and had kept them close to their encampments, and it was unsafe to stray out of them; that it would not be possible to go far into the country, at a distance from the victuallers [i.e. ships] for from them we must depend for our bread.'[17] All this confirmed Burrard's worst fears. It seemed to him that Sir Arthur had got himself into a very difficult position, but Sir Arthur then reported that he had given orders for a further advance 'early next morning.' Now Sir Harry was really alarmed. It was now quite clear that Sir Arthur was the rash young man that he had feared. 'The decision I had to come to appeared most serious in its consequences: I gave the subject every consideration in my power, and decided that the army should halt. The strength at which I had calculated the force of the enemy in and about Lisbon; his power of better equipment than ours; his great superiority of cavalry, with our almost total want of it; the reinforcements of all kinds which he could draw from his headquarters, with the more safety and the more ease as we approached his resources, were considerations, I trust, sufficiently weighty, to authorise me to wait for the reinforcements which were at hand. Had our arms in the progress of advancing received a check, it is impossible to calculate the disasters to which it might have exposed them.'[18]

Wellesley tried to reason with him. In Torrens' words, he 'observed that he thought it of the utmost importance to push forward by way of Mafra, with a view to turning the enemy's left flank, and to endeavour to bring the French army to the issue of a battle in the field as near to Lisbon as possible, that we might avail ourselves of the short distance from the Tagus, by following up the victory, so as to prevent the French from crossing that river. And he further stated, that he was desirous of this contest taking place near to Lisbon, having an actual survey of all the country in the vicinity of that town.'[19] Sir Arthur further pointed out that every day in which they waited in their present position would throw an additional strain on the supply situation, that 'the army was so near the French army that one of the two must attack,'[20] and that 'if we did not move to attack the French, they would attack us.'[21] Even if the French did not attack 'they would fortify their positions between our army and Lisbon during the delay in our march,' and that there 'the badness of the roads, as well as the narrowness of them, would render the turning of the enemy's flank in any position very difficult.'[22]

Nothing would shake Sir Harry's determination. 'Sir Harry Burrard repeated that he thought it advisable to bring down Sir John Moore's corps, to render certain those operations which appeared to him to be doubtful.'[23]

This brought the discussion round to Wellesley's plan for sending Moore's corps to Santarem. He explained his reasons at length. 'I had always considered possession of Lisbon and of the Tagus to be the great object of the campaign both to us and to the French; that for this object a battle would be fought in the field, in which I thought I had every reason to expect success; and that the enemy would after this battle endeavour to retire across the Tagus to Elvas, or along the right bank of the Tagus towards Almeida. . . . The occupation of Santarem by Sir John Moore's corps, was calculated to cut off these lines of retreat. . . . As I set out with the certainty that the French would not, nay, could not abandon Lisbon and the Tagus without fighting a battle for these possessions, I may conclude that after the battle they would have been so much weakened as that Sir John Moore's corps would have been a match for them; and at all events it is not to be supposed that, if this battle had been fought, they would not have been followed by a part, if not the whole, of the army which, in this supposition, would have defeated them. Indeed . . . I considered this position [Santarem] so little dangerous, and at the same time so advantageous, that if the brigades of Brigadier-Generals Acland and Anstruther had been equipped to act independently of any other body of troops, I should have ordered those brigades to occupy it.'[24]

To Sir Harry such arguments merely confirmed his belief that Wellesley was irresponsible and that, not content with putting his own corps into a position of great danger, he was intent on persuading Burrard to put Moore's corps into another. He reiterated his decision and sat down and wrote to Moore without further delay:

'Sir,
    Circumstances seeming to render it expedient that the force here should be reinforced by the addition of the troops under your orders, I request that you will proceed with them to this anchorage as soon as possible. Should you have commenced your disembarkation at Mondego, it will be better for that part of the corps which still remains on board should sail for this place, without waiting for the re-embarkation of those that may have landed, which, I conclude, will be the smallest part of your force.
    'If a part only of your force comes forward, I have to request that you will leave a junior officer to bring forward the

remainder, as I am desirous that you should join me yourself as soon as you can.'[25]

This order to Moore seems to show that Sir Harry's judgment had now gone completely to pieces. Given that he persisted in overestimating his opponent's resources and that he assumed that even if Junot was defeated near the sea nothing could be done by Wellesley's corps to molest his retreat, the refusal to move Moore to Santarem could be justified. He could argue that it exposed the army to defeat in detail. His previous orders to Moore, to form a firm base at Leiria in case Wellesley was defeated, were comprehensible as a counsel of despair. The new orders ensured that Moore's corps could perform no useful function at the crucial moment. With Moore disembarking at Mondego, as he had been ordered, it must take at least a week for him to re-embark, sail down to Maçeira and disembark again.* If the light winds and calms persisted it could take very much more. If, on the other hand, the wind rose considerably, as the naval officers expected it to do at the end of August, it would be impossible to land troops and horses on Maçeira beach. If Wellesley's corps defeated Junot, they would not need Moore's men, except at Santarem. If they were defeated they would now not have even their firm base at Leiria.

It is charitable to suppose that Burrard fell into the mistake of so many commanders, at all levels, before and since, of assuming that the enemy would keep still until the plans for his destruction were complete. It is fair to add that Sir Harry was right in thinking that Wellesley had underestimated the total French strength in Portugal. There were 24,000 French effective in the country compared with Wellesley's maximum estimate of 18,000. Since, however, Junot considered that many more troops were needed to overawe Lisbon than either Burrard or Wellesley had allowed, his field force, rather more than 13,000 was about the strength that Wellesley had expected to have to meet with

* Wellesley estimated to Burrard that it would take ten days. In fact Moore's corps was complete on shore at the end of the ninth day.

his own augmented corps of almost 17,000 rank and file exclusive of Portuguese. It must also have been a factor in Burrard's mind that if the army, without Moore's corps, won a victory, Wellesley would inevitably get the credit. If, as Burrard feared, the army was defeated, he, Burrard, would be held responsible.

By the time that Burrard had finished writing his letter it was almost dark and he gave the letter to Sir Arthur with a request that it should be sent overland to Moore at Mondego. Wellesley then went ashore but Sir Harry stayed afloat. It is frequently asserted or implied that he did so for the sake of his personal comfort.[26] Colour is lent to this interpretation by the fact that during the evening he exchanged his cramped quarters in the sloop for the greater comfort of H.M.S. *Alfred*, a ship of the line. This is a misreading of Burrard's motives. It is in any case unlikely that anyone not bred to the sea would not, after twenty-six days on board, have taken the first opportunity of leaving the overcrowding and stench of a man-of-war even for the meanest Portuguese hovel, but Sir Harry was determined to write another letter to Moore.

The letter which he had already dispatched was written in Sir Arthur's presence and, as a matter of common courtesy, he would have shown it to him before sealing it. That letter had, therefore, been written in the most formal and matter of fact fashion. The second letter was a personal letter starting 'My dear General' rather than, as before, 'Sir'. In this letter he told Moore, as he had not done in the first, that he had talked to Wellesley, and that Junot 'with nearly his whole force' was in position at Torres Vedras. Stress was laid on the shortages of cavalry and artillery horses and the lack of camp-kettles among the newly arrived troops. There is explicit urgency about every thing he ordered and, although there was no open criticism of Wellesley, the impression, when taken with the letter of the previous day, was that the army was in a critical position and only the most strenuous measures could extricate it. It added nothing to his previous orders but it would sound well if it came to a court martial.

Having sent this second letter off by the *Brazen*, Sir Harry went to bed. He made no arrangement for night signals should anything occur during the hours of darkness, but he had arranged with Wellesley that he would land in the morning as soon as horses for his use arrived on the beach. He told his two aides-de-camp to go ashore early in the morning, walk to Vimeiro and look for horses or mules for themselves. He was comfortably certain that nothing would happen in the immediate future and, in any case, 'I suppose communication could at any time be held between the beach and the *Alfred*, where I remained that night.'[27] It was, after all, only three miles from Wellesley's head-quarters to the beach and a mile and a half from the beach to the ship.

Meanwhile Wellesley had ridden back to Vimeiro. On arrival he issued a 'Night Pass Order'* to his eight brigades: 'The army will halt tomorrow. The men to sleep accoutred tonight, in readiness to turn out, and to be under arms at three o'clock in the morning.'[28]

* i.e. an order to be passed from one brigade to another, rather than a copy being sent to each brigade.

References

Chapter 5. 'I decided that the Army should halt'

1   Cintra 158. Evidence of HB
2   ib 158–59
3   Moore Diary ii 253
4   Cintra 159. Evidence of HB
5   Moore Diary ii 253
6   ib
7   ib
8   Cintra 160. Evidence of HB
9   ib
10 ib 161
11 Cintra 548. HB to Moore, 19 Aug '08
12 SD vi 119. General Order of 18 Aug '08
13 Cintra 58. Evidence of Captain Malcolm R.N.
14 Neale: letter of 20 Aug '08
15 Cintra 43. Evidence of AW
16 SD vi 120. General Order of 20 Aug '08

17 Cintra 162. Evidence of HB
18 ib
19 Cintra 195. Evidence of Colonel Torrens
20 Cintra 184. Evidence of Captain Lord Burghersh
21 Cintra 196. Evidence of Colonel Torrens
22 ib
23 Cintra 195. Evidence of Colonel Torrens
24 Cintra 199–200. Evidence of AW
25 Cintra 550. HB to Moore, 20 Aug '08
26 Cf. Oman i 250
27 Cintra 168. Evidence of HB
28 SD vi 121 Night Pass Order, 20 Aug '08

'Sir Harry, Now is Your

I N the small hours of 21st August, a standing patrol of the
Twentieth Light Dragoons which was stationed to the south
of Vimeiro was told by a peasant that a heavy French column,
which he estimated at 20,000 men, was advancing towards the
British position. This was reported to General Fane, commanding
the outposts. He immediately put his brigade on the alert and
relayed the news to Wellesley. Sir Arthur was disinclined to
believe the story and, while approving Fane's action, told Fane
that 'you may allow the men to fall out and lie down; but they
must sleep accoutred. Before I had heard this report I had
ordered two 9-pounders to your ground, and since I have received
it I have desired that you may continue to send patrols to your
front, and that you will do me the favour to let me know if
they should report anything extraordinary.'[1]

Not long afterwards the dragoon patrol heard in the still night
air the clatter of hooves and the rumble of guns and limbers as
Junot's army crossed the wooden bridge over the Maçeira river
on the road from Torres Vedras to Lourinha. The patrol commander, Serjeant Landsheit, at once reported to Fane who sent
him straight off to Wellesley. 'I rode to the house where the
general dwelt, and being admitted, I found him, with a large
staff, all seated on a long table in the hall, back to back, swinging

Time to Advance'

their legs to and fro, like men on whose minds not a shadow of anxiety rested. The general himself . . . closely examined me, and told me I had done my duty well. He then desired me to go below and get something to eat and drink from his servant, which I did, though not till I had heard him give his orders, in a calm, clear and cheerful voice. They were in substance these: "Now, gentlemen, go to your stations; but let there be no noise made – no sounding of bugles or beating of drums. Get your men quietly under arms, and desire all the outposts to be on the alert." [2]

When dawn broke all was quiet and Sir Arthur rode along the position with Brigadier-General Anstruther. As a position to cover the landing beach at Maçeira, the Vimeiro ridge is admirable. West of the village it rises steeply from the sea and runs at right-angles to it for more than a mile and a half to a point north of Vimeiro village, where it is cut through by the Maçeira river, running in a steep cleft. As far as the cleft, the river is steep-faced and rises, at its highest point, Valongo hill, to more than three-hundred feet. From the crest of this, the Valongo ridge, there is a clear view towards the south and, especially, towards the south-east, the direction from which the French were advancing.

East of the cleft, the ridge slopes away to the north-east, a convenient natural formation, forming what in military terms is known as a 'refused flank', one on which the defence is held back but which can be reinforced easily across the base of the triangle if the enemy is seen to be making the much longer approach march necessary to reach it. This part of the ridge, which has as its main feature Mariano hill, is a spur running down from high ground to the north. The forward slope of this ridge, Mariano ridge, is gentler than that of Valongo ridge and the road from Vimeiro to Lourinha runs up and along it, bifurcating at the hamlet of Ventosa, from where one branch runs either side to the crest of Mariano hill. The approach to the ridge is, however, made difficult to troops in formation by a dry watercourse, running close to the hamlet of Toledo. The two ridges made an admirable defensive position on which Wellesley was to fight his first defensive battle and gave him a chance to try for the first time what was to become his most famous tactical device, that of holding his infantry behind the crest, hidden from the enemy and sheltered from their artillery, until the enemy infantry could come close enough for the British to make a short advance and destroy their opponents with their devastating volleys at fifty yards or less.

In front of Vimeiro village there is a low hill, covered with scrub and a few small pines, which, in normal circumstances, would serve as an outwork which could be relinquished under pressure without compromising the main position. Unfortunately, Wellesley had been forced to put his main park of transport, with its load of invaluable supplies, in and around the village. The roads, or rather tracks, behind the village were inadequate for such a mass of vehicles. With the army due to march off in the small hours of the following morning the risk of having the transport in front of the main position had seemed acceptable. Now that Burrard had ordered the army on to the defensive, the park seemed uncomfortably exposed and Vimeiro hill a strong-point that must be held at all costs. Certainly, with the advance of the enemy reported, it would be impractical to attempt to move the mass of carts, bullocks and mules with their excitable and undisciplined Portuguese drivers through the defile of the cleft. That could only lead to chaos. It remained true, however, that if the French got in among the transport the campaign would come to a stop whatever the result of the battle.

The defence of Vimeiro hill Wellesley entrusted to his best troops. Brigadier-General Henry Fane* commanded and had with him his own brigade, 1,100 rifles of the Sixtieth and Ninety-Fifth and nearly 900 muskets of the 1st battalion Fiftieth. He also commanded Anstruther's† brigade, the strongest in the army with more than 2,700 muskets, comprising the 2nd battalions of the Ninth, Forty-Third, Fifty-Second and Ninety-Seventh. While all these were good battalions, Fane was particularly fortunate in having under command the Forty-Third, Fifty-Second and Ninety-Fifth, all battalions which had been trained by Sir John Moore in his famous Light Brigade at Shorncliffe and were generally recognised as the finest infantry in the army. With Fane also were two batteries of guns, one of 9- and one of 6-pounders, two-thirds of the artillery with the army.

Almost all the rest of the infantry was drawn up on the Valongo ridge, the brigades of Rowland Hill,‡ Catlin Craufurd,§ Miles Nightingall,‖, Barnard Bowes,¶ and Ronald Ferguson,**

* Henry Fane (1778–1840) educ. Eton, subsequently one of Wellington's most trusted cavalry brigadiers.
† Robert Anstruther (1768–1809) educ. Westminster. Died of dysentry on day before Battle of Coruña and buried beside Sir John Moore.
‡ Rowland Hill (later Lord Hill) (1772–1842) Wellington's favourite divisional and corps commander in the Peninsular and Waterloo campaigns. Succeeded Wellington as Commander-in-Chief, 1825.
§ Catlin Craufurd (17??–1810), served at Coruña and returned to Peninsula in September 1809 only to die of sickness a year later.
‖ Miles Nightingall (1768–1829), a hypochondriac protégé of Lord Cornwallis. Wounded commanding 1st Division at Fuentes De Oñoro. Sought an Indian command (1810) finding Portugal brought on his 'old trouble' (unspecified).
¶ Barnard Bowes (17??–1812). Killed at the head of his brigade at the assault on the Salamanca forts, June 1812.
** Ronald Ferguson (1773–1841) MP, Kirkaldy Burghs, 1806–30. Left the Peninsula after Convention of Cintra.

in that order filling the whole stretch between the sea and the cleft. To the east of the cleft was only a single British battalion, the 1st battalion of the Fortieth, from Ferguson's brigade, with the Portuguese infantry in reserve. The cavalry, three squadrons of the Twentieth and two of Portuguese, were stationed under cover of Vimeiro hill where their standing patrols joined them as they were driven in.

It was Wellesley's firm conviction that Junot would attempt to break through the position on the Valongo ridge, aiming to get between the army and the landing beach. With this in mind he remarked to Anstruther, as they rode along the line that 'he thought the right flank rather thin of troops, and ordered Acland's* brigade, which had landed in the night, to be placed there in second line.'[3]

While Wellesley was making this final inspection of his army, Junot had halted his men, about four miles from Vimeiro village, to cook their breakfasts. This he could safely do as his cavalry was more than sufficient to protect him from surprise. Junot had many things to worry him – the seething discontent in Lisbon, open revolt in all the parts of Portugal out of reach of the bayonets of his garrisons, his lack of communication with Spain and France – but he was absolutely confident of his ability to beat the English. This confidence derived from two factors. The first was common to the whole French army, a belief in the invincibility of Napoleon's troops. There was much evidence to support this belief, especially to those, like Junot's army, who had not heard of Dupont's defeat at Bailen. The French had defeated every Continental army that had stood in their path and the British had made a particularly humiliating showing. Time and again they had landed armies on the Continent, only to re-embark them in more or less confusion as soon as the French had shown their strength. It was true that, two years earlier, they had landed in Italy and defeated General Reynier with equal numbers at Maida, but they had quickly re-embarked just

* Wroth Acland (1770–1816) Returned to England after Convention of Cintra and did not serve again in the Peninsula.

106

the same. The other factor was Junot's own character. It was not for nothing that he was known in the army as 'the Hurricane'. General Thiebault, his Chief-of-Staff, wrote of him that he 'was a clever man, a very clever man indeed; he was a man of education and, when he really applied his reasoning power, a man of sense and even of great judgment and sagacity. He was now thirty-seven years old; for fourteen years he had been aide-de-camp to the greatest general of modern times. . . . As far as preliminaries were concerned, no pupil ever copied his master better. But . . . Junot was headlong and fiery; he had no perseverance nor did he have the self-control without which mere fire is unimportant. Blindly courageous as a soldier, he had no comprehensive view, no foresight, no inspiration. In any kind of battle, the only thing he understood was shock action. He had no notion of tactics.'[4] Junot started the day with the belief that he could bludgeon his way through.

Junot's field force consisted of rather more than 13,000 men. Of these 10,500 were infantry, almost 2,000 were cavalry and there were twenty-three guns. He had, therefore, a great superiority in cavalry, four to one even if the Portuguese were counted on the allied side. With artillery he had twenty-three to eighteen, a comfortable margin. His infantry, however, was outnumbered by three to two, without counting the Portuguese contingent. Much of this inferiority was his own fault. He had left 6,500 men as a garrison for Lisbon and the Tagus forts. Half that number would have sufficed. Napoleon later observed that the city would be unlikely to rise unless Junot was defeated. If it did, and Junot returned victorious it could be easily, if bloodily, brought to order. To some extent he may have been the victim of Wellesley's deception plan which arranged for the red coats of his Veteran battalion to be seen in their transports hovering off the forts of Cascais and St Julian. The thought that he had over-insured in Lisbon occurred to him on 20th August, the day before the battle, and he sent for a further 1,200 men. Such was his confidence, however, that he was not prepared to postpone his attack for twenty-four hours so that they could join him.

His infantry was divided into five brigades, varying in strength between 1,000 and 3,000. Four of these were allocated in pairs to two divisions commanded by Generals Delaborde and Loison. The fifth brigade, the *élite* of the army, consisted of the grenadier companies of every battalion in Portugal grouped into four battalions and commanded by General Kellermann, son of Marshal Kellermann, the hero of Valmy in the Revolutionary wars. The grenadier brigade formed the reserve of infantry.

The French knowledge of Wellesley's strength was derived from Delaborde's view of the British army when it had deployed four days earlier at Roliça. Delaborde's reports had been reasonably accurate and Junot was under the impression that, with 13,000 men, he was attacking an army of roughly equal strength. For some reason, which has never been explained, his cavalry, although they had patrolled up to Maçeira beach, had failed to inform him that strong reinforcements had been landed. Wellesley had, in fact, a British strength of 16,788 of whom 240 were cavalry and 226 manned the eighteen guns. There were, in addition, 2,000 Portuguese. Oblivious of this, Junot proposed to launch his main attack at the British line, aiming to break through. If this succeeded one part of the British would be pinned against the sea, while the rest would have to retreat north-east. Vimeiro was no position from which to retreat. On Wellesley's right flank was the sea; to his rear was the French held fortress of Peniche. To re-embark over beaches swept by French fire would be impossible. The only escape route would be the road running north-east over the Mariano ridge. This Junot intended to block. By all contemporary French standards, the plan was feasible. Junot was fully confident that it would succeed. Wellesley, who knew the steadiness of British infantry, was equally certain that, on a position as strong as Vimeiro, it would not.

Vimeiro was the first of a long series of clashes between two rival schools of military thought, clashes that continued through Talavera, Busaco, Fuentes de Oñoro, Albuera, Salamanca, Vitoria, the Pyrenees, Toulouse and, supremely, Waterloo. Each of the two schools strove to make the best use of the principal contemporary weapon. This was the 'common musket', a crude, mass-produced weapon, its flintlock action exceedingly susceptible to misfiring, even in dry weather, and which was not accurate at a range of more than fifty yards.* The musket ball, however, was lethal far beyond the range at which it was accurate, up to at least three-hundred yards. It was, therefore, necessary to fire a great number of balls close together so that a proportion of them would be certain to hit the enemy. As reloading, even for a trained soldier, took from 12 to 15 seconds there was no recourse but for the infantry to fight in shoulder to shoulder formation and to fire their muskets in closely controlled volleys, either rank by rank or file by file. Thus, a vast number of balls could be fired and a proportion of the muskets were always kept loaded against an emergency. This problem faced both sides. The difference lay in the method of bringing the available fire power to bear. The classic doctrine was to arrange the available muskets in a three-deep line so that the muskets of the front two ranks† could be brought to bear on any enemy to their front. Such a formation was extremely difficult to manœuvre, as even a single full-strength battalion formed a line more than three hundred yards long and that of a brigade would stretch over half a mile. To fight so required a very high standard of drill and training, while the thinness of the line made it essential that the troops should be very steady under fire.

Up to the French Revolution every civilised army had fought in this way, but the French, without altering their drill books, had increasingly taken to using troops as human missiles, forming their battalions and brigades into heavy columns with a front of forty and a depth of eighteen ranks for each battalion. Frequently whole brigades advanced with their battalions one behind the other, so that there could be sixty or more ranks behind the

---

* The French and English muskets were very similar except that the English threw a somewhat larger ball. In both the misfire rate was two misfires in every thirteen balls fired in dry weather. In wet weather it was unlikely that any rounds could be fired.
† The rear rank of three could not fire without grave danger to those in front.

leading line of forty men. Sometimes the French used double column, with a front of eighty men and the remainder of the battalion in nine ranks behind them. Obviously this formation greatly reduced the fire power of a battalion since, again, only the front two ranks could fire, but, when the way had been cleared by a bold use of artillery and the sharpshooting of a cloud of *tirailleurs*, the momentum of the column could, and frequently did, carry it through the line of an enemy. This technique had been used with success against the Austrians, the Prussians, the Russians, the Spaniards and, on occasions, against the British. It was this Wellesley was referring to when he said (*see p.* 42) that he had heard that the French had 'a new system of strategy'.

The British had resolutely refused to adopt this system. Their army was, compared with Continental armies, a small one and its standard of drill was kept at a higher level than any other. Thus British battalions could perform the complicated evolutions needed to fight in line with a facility with which other armies could not compete. Moreover, the steadiness of British infantry, with their tradition for stubborn bravery going back to Minden, Blenheim, Agincourt and Hastings, made them ideally suitable for this type of fighting. The British response to the threat of the missile action of the French column had been two-fold. They had trained a high proportion of their infantry as light troops, to compete with and overwhelm the French *tirailleurs* and they had armed a proportion of them with rifles, accurate up to three-hundred yards.* For the bulk of their troops they had decided, contrary to their own drill books, to abandon the three-deep line for two deep. This made even greater demands on the steadiness of the men, demands that were always met, but it gave the enormous advantage that every musket could be brought to bear. Thus, a French battalion with a strength of 1,000 men advancing in single column with a front of forty men, could

---

* The French had experimented with rifles but, on Napoeon's orders they had all been withdrawn in 1807 as being too cumbersome. There was an element of truth in this as even a fully-trained rifleman could fire only two shots a minute.

fire only eighty muskets at their enemy, while a British battalion of the same strength could bring every one of their thousand muskets to bear, especially, as frequently happened, if the wing companies were inclined forward so that they could fire into the flanks of the column. There could be no doubt that in theory the British formation was the most effective but fifteen years of French experience had shown them that they could break through.

*   *   *

Having breakfasted, Junot made a reconnaissance of the British position. He took only a cursory look at it but it was sufficient to show him that a break-through over the Valongo ridge was impractical. He, therefore, decided that his main attack must be launched through Vimeiro village. To this he allocated three brigades, both the brigades of Loison's division and one from Delaborde. Delaborde's second brigade, accompanied by a regiment of dragoons and six guns, were ordered to make a wide sweep round to the north-east, where it was to take up a position blocking the British escape route on the Lourinha road. This brigade, commanded by Brennier, was the largest in the army, over 3,000 strong, and had been somewhat shaken by the rough handling it had received at Roliça.

The main attack was to be delivered by two brigades, one from each division, in first line, with Loison's second brigade in second line. The brigade of grenadiers was held in reserve to exploit success through the cleft in the ridge.

There was no chance of concealing the French movements in daylight. An hour before the French army came in sight, the British on the crest of the Valongo ridge could see clouds of dust as men, horses and guns moved over the sandy country. From the directions in which they moved Wellesley was able to deduce first, that he had been wrong in thinking that Junot would try to drive straight for the beaches over the Valongo ridge and, second, that a substantial force was attempting to turn his left flank. He immediately redisposed his forces. Five brigades were marched off the Valongo ridge, leaving it to the care of Hill's brigade of three strong battalions. The main force moved across the cleft, on the eastern side of which Acland's brigade was now stationed. Three brigades marched up the Lourinha road to a point a little short of Ventosa, where they formed with two brigades in line, astride the road and one in reserve. The remaining brigade, Craufurd's, of two battalions, acted as a link between them and Acland. Fane and Anstruther remained on Vimeiro hill.

Although the British redeployment was carried out, as far as possible, in dead ground behind the ridge, Junot realised that a great shift of strength was taking place from right to left. This alarmed him. Brennier's brigade in position across the Lourinha road would be sufficient to check a retreating army, already shaken and being pressed by the French cavalry in its rear, but, with Wellesley moving strong forces towards him, Brennier would be isolated and vulnerable. In what seems to have been a panic measure, Junot ordered Solignac's brigade, the second strongest in the army, to march after Brennier, who had a long start, and act in his support. Solignac's brigade was that previously intended to act in second line to the two brigades assigned to storm Vimeiro village and hill. Inexcusably, no message was sent to Brennier warning him to expect the assistance of Solignac.

By this move Junot threw away any chance he might have had of achieving success on that day. Not only did he so arrange things that each of his two attacks were delivered by two brigades each drawn from a different division, but he completely failed to co-ordinate the two formations attacking on his right. Worst of all, he fatally weakened the main attack. It is improbable that, even with three brigades assaulting Vimeiro, he could have broken through the cleft, but, with the larger force, he might have reached the exposed transport park and crippled the British ability to continue the campaign. As it was, both attacks failed.

The French found his behaviour inexplicable. 'Some thought that during the outdoor breakfast of which we had just been partaking, at which the general had drunk various wines and

112

screen and, when it seemed inevitable that they would be overwhelmed, the bugle-horns sounded the 'Fire and Retire' and the Greenjackets doubled to the flanks and thence to the rear. Both the forward British brigadiers showed a tendency to send out troops to cover the retreat of the Riflemen. Anstruther sent out the light company of the Ninety-Seventh and three companies of the Fifty-Second. Seeing this, Wellesley told his Military Secretary 'to ride as fast as I could to General Anstruther and General Fane, and to convey to them his orders that they should not move from the position which they occupied, . . . without further orders from Sir Arthur. On my arrival at that position, I found that General Fane had advanced a little way in front, and was engaged with some French light troops. I followed him and delivered those orders, and he consequently retired; this was about half past nine in the morning.'[6]

It was a mixed blessing for the French when the Riflemen cleared the front. Colonel Robe† was able to open fire with his twelve guns, the round shot tearing great lanes through the French columns while, over their heads, the French experienced for the first time the bursts of Major Shrapnel's spherical case shot, which, wrote Wellesley to its inventor, 'had the best effect'.[7] The French, nevertheless, pressed on in the most gallant fashion. They came on, said Wellesley in later life, 'with more confidence, and seemed to feel their way less than I always found them to do afterwards.'[8] The attacks of the two brigades reached the British position almost simultaneously. On the British right Anstruther was assailed by Charlot's brigade. Anstruther had drawn up his battalions with 'the 97th in line in front, in prolongation of the front of General Fane's brigade; 52nd in line in echelon to the flank of the 97th; 9th in open column behind, on the left flank of the 52nd; 43rd in open column behind the right flank of the 97th.'[9] Charlot's men advanced towards their left flank in column of march and, about nine-

---

† William Robe (1765–1820) Commander, Royal Artillery in this campaign and subsequently in the later campaign of 1812. Wounded on retreat from Burgos, October 1812, and invalided home. By the contemporary standard of senior gunner officers he was not inefficient.

115

hundred yards from the front of the Ninety-Seventh, deployed to their left into column of attack fronting the Ninety-Seventh. They advanced to a line of pines about a hundred-and-fifty yards from the British front when Anstruther 'ordered the 97th, who were concealed behind a dip in the ground, to rise and fire; after firing two or three rounds they [97th] began to advance from the position, and finding it impossible to stop them without great risk, I ordered the 52nd to support them on their right, and if possible to turn the left of the enemy. This they did very dexterously; while the 97th made a vigorous attack in front. The enemy soon gave way, and was pursued to the skirts of the wood beyond, beyond which his superiority made it imprudent to advance. I rallied the 97th, and leaving strong piquets in the wood, brought them back to the position: the 9th remained in reserve but was very little engaged.'[10]

On Anstruther's left, Thomières' brigade, which was stronger than Charlot's, had a more serious encounter with Fane who, with his Riflemen still coming in to form as his reserve, had only a single battalion in line to oppose him. This was the Fiftieth, 945 strong, 'not', in Wellesley's words, 'a good-looking regiment, but devilish steady.' Its Lieutenant-Colonel, George Walker, a loyalist American, recalled in a memorandum written four years later that 'a massive column of the enemy in close order, supported by seven pieces of cannon, made a rapid advance towards the hill, and although much shaken by the steady fire of the artillery, after a short pause behind a hedge to recover, it again continued to advance; till Lieut.-Col. Robe R.A., no longer able to use the guns, considered them lost. Up to this time the 50th had remained at ordered arms, but it was impossible on the ground on which it stood to contend against so superior a force and Colonel Walker, having observed that the enemy's column inclined to the left, proposed to Brigadier-General Fane to attempt to turn its flank by a wheel of the right wing. Permission for this having been obtained, this wing was immediately thrown into echelon of half companies of about four paces to the left. The rapidity, however, of the enemy's advance, and their having already opened a confused though very hot fire from the flank of their column – though only two companies of the wing were yet formed – these were so nearly in contact with and bearing upon the angle of the column that Colonel Walker, thinking no time was to be lost, ordered an immediate volley and charge. The result exceeded his most sanguine expectations. The angle was instantly broken, and the drivers of the three guns advanced in front, alarmed at the fire in their rear, cutting the traces of their horses, and rushing back with them, created great confusion which, by the time the three outer companies could arrive to take part in the charge, became general. Then this immense mass, so threatening in its appearance a few minutes before, became in an instant an ungovernable mob, carrying off its officers and flying like a flock of sheep, almost without resistance. On clearing a small wood, Colonel Walker, observing a party of cavalry drawn up on a small plain, threatening his flank, deemed it necessary to put a stop to the pursuit.'[11]

Junot's attack had achieved nothing. There was no breakthrough, not an inch of ground had been gained, but seven guns had been lost, Delaborde and Charlot had been wounded and the two assaulting brigades were unfit for further immediate service. His only reserve was his 2,000 grenadiers, the *élite* of his army. These he unhesitatingly threw into the battle. This time his aim was not directly to assault Vimeiro hill but to seize Vimeiro village in its rear. To do this he sent two battalions against the Fiftieth, now supported by their Riflemen, and endeavoured to turn their left with the other two battalions led by General Kellermann. The Fiftieth were in a very dangerous position but fortunately the brigade commanders on either flank unhesitatingly sent Fane reinforcements. From his right Anstruther, finding himself not attacked, sent the Forty-Third behind Fane's brigade, to cover the village, in the front houses of which they put two companies. From the left Kellermann's column came under heavy fire from Acland's brigade and Acland sent down two rifle and two light companies closely to engage his right. The Fiftieth fought off their direct assailants as gallantly as they had the previous attack, but Kellermann's two battalions proved of sterner stuff. Advancing in column of platoons, on a front of sixteen men, with rank after rank in rear, they battled their way through a hail of shrapnel, rifle fire and musketry, right up to the walls of Vimeiro village. 'They were', said a participant, 'fine looking young men, wearing red shoulder knots and tremendous-looking moustaches.'[12] Gallant as they were, the odds against them were too great. There was a brief, bitter bayonet fight around the village cemetery and the French began to fall back.

Having disposed of their immediate assailants, Fane's brigade was restive to charge. Their general had trouble restraining them. ' "Don't be too eager, men", he said coolly, as if we were on drill parade in England; "I don't want you to advance just yet." A man named Brotherwood, of the 95th, at this moment rushed up to the general, and presented him with a green feather, which he had torn out of the cap of a French light infantryman he had killed. "God bless you, general", he said; "wear this for the sake of the 95th." I saw the general take the feather and stick it in his cocked hat. The next minute he gave the word to charge, and down came the whole line.'[13]

All this time the Twentieth Light Dragoons had been waiting for their chance. 'Colonel Taylor who commanded us, repeatedly asked leave to charge, but was on each occasion held back by the assurance that the proper moment was not yet come; till at last General Fane rode up and exclaimed, "Now, Twentieth, now we want you. At them, lads, and let them see what you are made of." Then came the word, "threes about and forward," and we swept round the elbow of the hill and the battle lay before us. As we emerged up the slope, we were directed to form in half squadrons, the 20th in the centre, the Portuguese cavalry on the flanks. . . . "Now, Twentieth, now!" shouted Sir Arthur, while his staff clapped their hands and gave us a cheer, the sound of which was still in our ears when we put our horses to their speed. The Portuguese likewise pushed forward, but through the dust which entirely enveloped us the enemy threw in a fire, which seemed to have the effect of paralysing altogether our handsome allies. Right and left they pulled up as if by a word of command, and we never saw more of them until the battle was over. But we went very differently to work. In an instant we were in the heart of the French cavalry, cutting and hacking, and upsetting men and horses in the most extraordinary manner possible until they broke and fled in every direction, and then we fell upon the infantry. . . . Though scattered, as always happens by the shock of a charge, we still kept laying about us, till our white leather breeches, our hands, arms and swords were all besmeared with blood. Moreover, as the enemy gave way we continued to advance, amid a cloud of dust so thick, that to see beyond the distance of those immediately about yourself was impossible.'[14]

The Light Dragoons had made a magnificent charge but, as almost always happened with British cavalry in the Peninsula, they went too far. Outnumbered by five to one it could only be a question of time before the French cavalry counter-attacked. Scattered as they were, they were an easy prey to fresh French squadrons and they were fortunate to be able to straggle back to the British lines with no more loss than twenty-one killed, twenty-four wounded and eleven prisoners. Colonel Taylor was among the killed.

The charge of the Twentieth Dragoons was the end of the action in the centre. Junot had no unbroken infantry with which to attack. Wellesley had to reorganise and clear his left before he could advance. It was about half past ten – only two and a half hours since the first shots had been fired by the skirmishers. Almost simultaneously the action flared up on the left flank.

With his main attack broken, there was no point in Junot proceeding with his flanking movement but there was no time now to stop it. While it provided the French with the nearest they got to a success that day it was all but a foregone conclusion, the more so by Junot's fault. The two French brigades attacked without co-ordination and lessened their already slim chance of success. The situation was made worse by the fact that Brennier's brigade seems to have gone north until it struck the Vimeiro-Lourinha road and then turned south-west, thus taking a very long way round. Thus Solignac, who marched up the Mariano

119

ridge near the hamlet of Toledo,* came into action first. With his three battalions in parallel columns and preceded by a thick skirmishing line he struck north for Ventosa. He could see few British troops ahead, only the skirmishers of Ferguson's light companies, and the French advanced quickly and confidently with their guns in the intervals of the columns. Ahead of them, behind the crest, were seven British battalions which were quickly re-forming to their right with their backs to the Lourinha-Vimeiro road. In front were Ferguson's three battalions, the Thirty-Sixth, Seventy-First and Fortieth with, on their left, the Eighty-Second of Nightingall's brigade. In second line were Bowes' two battalions, the Sixth and Thirty-Second, with Nightingall's remaining unit, the Twenty-Ninth.

Before Solignac realised what was in front of him, it was too late. The British front line, with 3,000 muskets, advanced to the crest and, at a range of less than a hundred yards, poured a volley into the French columns, the flanking battalions inclining their outer wings to pour their fire into the flanks of the French columns. Then they reloaded and, in complete silence, started to advance down the slope. 'The enemy retired before us', wrote Ferguson's aide-de-camp. 'A part of them rallied but General Ferguson hurra'ed the 36th, a very weak though fine regiment, to charge, which was done in great style three successive times,

---

* The directions from which Solignac and later Brennier attacked are hard to determine. The brigades of Ferguson, Nightingall and Bowes were originally formed by Wellesley astride the Mariano ridge facing the village of Ventosa, i.e. facing uphill towards the north-east. All the authorities agree that Solignac attacked uphill and could see only the skirmishes in front of the main British line until it was too late to draw back. It follows, therefore, that he must have attacked from the Toledo valley, probably along the Toledo-Ventosa track, rather than attacking from Ventosa (as shown in the maps of Fortescue, Oman and Weller) which would have been downhill, with the British clearly visible from some distance. Brennier, on the other hand, attacked downhill. He probably came down the Lourinha-Vimeiro road to Ventosa and struck off right into the ravine west of the Toledo-Ventosa track where Solignac had abandoned his guns.

120

till, as they were much thinned, and in some disorder from their rapid advance, I was sent back to hasten the support, which was far behind, the gallant little regiment forming to rally again under the cover of a hedge of American aloes, though much pressed. I had just returned in time to join the 71st, who were charging six pieces of artillery that were retiring, and the fire at this time was really tremendous.'[15] The Seventy-First went forward to the sound of the pipes. Piper M'Kayes, a 'remarkably handsome fellow . . . was wounded in the lower part of the belly and fell. He recovered himself almost immediately and continued to play on the ground till quite exhausted.'[16] At this renewed onslaught the French broke and Ferguson pursued them with the Thirty-Sixth and Fortieth, driving them eastwards, away from Junot and the main body. The captured guns were left in the care of the Seventy-First and Eighty-Second.

It was only a short time later that Brennier completed his long flank march. He was advancing south-west on the Lourinha-Vimeiro road when, having passed through Ventosa, he saw in the re-entrant to his left the captured guns with the two battalions standing at ease round them. He immediately attacked downhill with his dragoons covering his flanks. The Seventy-First and Eighty-Second were taken by surprise, driven away from their booty and up the westward slope of the re-entrant. At the top, however, they rallied and quickly re-formed. Then, supported by the Twenty-Ninth which had so far not been engaged, they charged downhill in their turn. There was a short moment of desperate fighting before the French broke and, covered by their dragoons, ran for their lives, leaving General Brennier wounded and a prisoner.

It was now about noon and every French battalion present had been not only engaged but broken. The men of the brigades of Brennier and Solignac were trying to escape eastwards. The main body was retiring of its own accord to the south-east. For the moment they were useless as a military body. Nor did Junot make any effort to rally them. According to General Thiebault, 'as soon as retreat became necessary, Junot disappeared without giving orders to anyone. . . . [He] got into a carriage with

Madame Foy, whose husband had just been wounded, and drove right through our whole column.'[17]

To Wellesley the battle was 'but half done'.[18] The British had suffered only 720 casualties. They had in their hands 300 prisoners and all but nine of the French guns. Three brigades, those of Hill, Bowes and Craufurd, had not fired a shot and of the rest only the Forty-Third, Fiftieth, Seventy-First and Eighty-Second had suffered serious casualties. The French were beaten but not destroyed, but they could be destroyed if the British moved fast enough. By wheeling forward from the right, using Hill's brigade followed by those of Anstruther, Fane and Acland, they could reach Torres Vedras before the French could get to that vital defile. Once Torres Vedras was held the French could only reach Lisbon by crossing the rugged, roadless country of the *massif* of Monte Junta. If that happened Lisbon must fall and Junot forced to make the best of his way back to the frontier, beset by a hostile populace. Wellesley gave the preliminary orders for such a move. Unfortunately he was no longer his own master.

At half-past-eight in the morning Sir Harry Burrard had still been on board H.M.S. *Alfred*. At that time he saw three horses led down to the beach and he was rowed ashore with his chief staff officers, Brigadier-General Clinton* and Colonel Murray.† 'I met an officer near the surf, who told me that he was sent by Sir Arthur Wellesley to inform me that large bodies of the enemy were seen moving to the left of the position.'[19] The three senior officers rode up to the battle and reached Vimeiro at about ten o'clock, when the grenadier brigade was attacking on and around Vimeiro hill. At the top of the hill, 'we found Sir Arthur who,

---

* Henry Clinton (1771–1829) younger son of the Henry Clinton who had commanded in the American war. Educ. Eton. MP for Boroughbridge 1808–18. Adjutant-General to Moore at Coruña. Commanded 6th division in Peninsula 1812–14 and 2nd division at Waterloo.

† George Murray (1772–1846) Educ. Edinburgh University and R. Military College. Was Wellington's Quartermaster-General in the Peninsula 1809–14 with a break in 1812. Secretary of State for the Colonies, 1828–30. Edited Marlborough's Dispatches.

in a few words, explained to me the position occupied by the army, and the steps taken to beat the enemy, who were then obviously attempting to turn our left. I had reason to be perfectly satisfied with his disposition, and the means he proposed to repulse them, and I directed him to go on with an operation he had so happily and so well begun.'[20] 'My proceedings were those, as I conceive, of an officer, who directed his junior to pursue or carry into effect some operation; and I directed my staff to assist in every way they could.'[21]

The defeat of Solignac and Brennier on the left flank seemed to Sir Harry to mark the end of the battle and he, thereupon, took the command of the army into his own hands. Before Wellesley could give the executive order to advance he must, therefore, seek Burrard's consent. He rode up to him, acompanied by his Military Secretary who reported the interview, and said, ' "Sir Harry, now is your time to advance, the enemy are completely beaten, and we shall be in Lisbon in three days. We have a large body of troops which have not been in action. Let us move from the right on the road to Torres Vedras, and I will follow them [the French] with the left." Sir Harry Burrard replied that he thought a great deal had been done very much to the credit of the troops, but that he did not think it advisable to move off the ground in pursuit of the enemy. Sir Arthur remarked that the troops were perfectly ready to advance, having provisions already cooked in their haversacks, according to the orders of the day before; . . . and there was plenty of ammunition, that the mules with the reserve of musket ammunition were in rear of the brigades, that we had an abundance of stores and plenty of provisions.'[22]

Sir Harry, in his own words, 'answered that I saw no reason for altering my former resolution of not advancing, and, as far as my recollection goes, I added that the same reasoning which before had determined me to wait for the reinforcements had still its full force in my judgment and opinions. . . . During the engagement I had frequent opportunities of observing the inability of our artillery horses for celerity of movement, or more work, the more to be lamented, as we had little or any cavalry.

I had received a report from an officer of the 20th Light Dragoons that the detachment was taken or cut to pieces, except himself and a few more who had charged through. In the morning, I had observed the commissariat, on my way from the shore, in confusion; they were loading with an intention, I suppose, of seeking safety as they were exposed to fire, and it was with much difficulty that my aide-de-camp got through them.'[23]

Sir Arthur had no option but to accept this ruling but, a few minutes later, an opportunity occurred to re-open the question. Captain Mellish, aide-de-camp to General Ferguson, arrived with a message from his general that he had the whole of Solignac's brigade penned in a ravine but that he could not make them prisoners without making a short further advance. This he sought permission to do but Burrard refused to sanction any move forward. In his view the army already occupied a position more extensive than their strength warranted. He peremptorily ordered Ferguson back to the original position and gave orders for the troops to encamp. Solignac escaped.

Sir Arthur 'turned his horse's head, and with a cold contemptuous bitterness, said aloud to his aide-de-camp, "You may think about dinner, for there is nothing more for soldiers to do this day." '[24]

References

Chapter 6. 'Sir Harry, Now is your time to advance'

1 SD vi 120. AW to Fane, 20 Aug '08
2 Hussar i 265
3 Wyldmem 3. Anstruther's Journal
4 Thiebault ii 208–09
5 ib
6 Cintra 197. Evidence of Torrens
7 SD vi 286. AW to Shrapnel, 16 June '09
8 Croker ii 122
9 Wyldmem 3. Anstruther's Journal
10 ib
11 Memorandum dated 17 Oct '12 by Colonel Walker. q. in Fyler *History of the 50th (Queen's Own) Regiment*

12 Harris
13 ib
14 Hussar i 267
15 Warre 32
16 ib 35
17 Thiebault ii 209
18 Croker ii 122
19 Cintra 168. Evidence of Burrard
20 ib 164
21 ib 169
22 Cintra 197. Evidence of Torrens
23 Cintra 165. Evidence of Burrard
24 Sherer 43

CHAPTER 7

'A Very Extraordinary

I T had taken more than three weeks for Castlereagh's letter appointing Sir Hew Dalrymple to the chief command of the British troops 'for the present', to reach him at Gibraltar. It was six more days before Sir Hew, on 13th August, embarked aboard the frigate *Phoebe* and 'by the first fair wind after my appointment, passed the straits; the same night I communicated with Lord Collingwood off Cadiz.'[1] Seldom has a Commander-in-Chief set out with less information about the situation he was going to find. Ever since he had heard, on 31st July, that Sir Hew was to take over the command Wellesley had punctiliously sent him copies of all his dispatches but, owing to the vagaries of the winds, none had reached him. From Admiral Collingwood Dalrymple learned little. Word had been received at Cadiz that the French had evacuated Madrid and were concentrating around Segovia. The news from Portugal was scant and a fortnight out of date. 'Lord Collingwood informed me of Sir Arthur Wellesley's corps having landed, or being about to land at Mondego Bay, a place, as his Lordship described it, where troops might in favourable weather disembark, but which afforded no protection or security for shipping with any weather which could create the surf on the shore for which the coast is remarkable. . . . I

126

Paper'

felt strongly impressed with the belief that Lieutenant-General Sir Arthur Wellesley would have to contend with the whole force of the French army until the arrival of the promised reinforcements.'[2]

On the 19th the *Phoebe* arrived off Lisbon and Dalrymple went on board Admiral Cotton's flagship. From Cotton he learned that Wellesley was ashore and marching along the coast road drawing his supplies from the fleet. The admiral also knew that Acland's force had sailed along the coast and was looking for an opportunity to land, although he did not know whether he had succeeded in doing so. Cotton clearly thought that the army was making rather heavy weather of the whole operation. 'Sir Charles seemed to have adopted a very moderate opinion of the French force, and did not appear to calculate upon any serious opposition.'[3]

Sir Hew was not impressed by Cotton's optimism. Since the proposal to invade Portugal had originated in the admiral's estimate of the French strength in Lisbon as being 4,000 men, he had some grounds for distrusting him. In any case Sir Hew was not given to optimism. In his view the idea of marching on Lisbon by the coast road was fundamentally unsound and likely to lead to catastrophe. 'From the opinion I had throughout entertained of the movement from Mondego Bay, by which every strong post, and every desirable line of communication was completely left to the enemy; without any prospect of support, or any other thing whatever for the British army to fall back upon in case of disaster, I conceived that whenever the enemy became aware of its situation and numbers, and determined on an attack, the battle on our part would be fought for existence.'[4] Sir Hew, before reaching the army, took an even more gloomy view of the situation than Sir Harry had done.

On the 21st the *Phoebe* spoke a sloop of war whose captain gave them 'a vague but, as it afterwards turned out, an exaggerated account' of Roliça. Towards evening, when it was nearly calm, a great many ships were sighted lying close to the shore and Captain Oswald R.N. sent his first-lieutenant ashore in a boat to gather intelligence. With the naval officer went one of Dalrymple's aides-de-camp with a message to Sir Arthur from Sir Hew 'that I was on my way to fall in with Sir Harry Burrard and the main body, but that, though I wished to be informed of his proceedings, I did not wish to interfere with his command.'[5] This was an extraordinary message. By his own admission Dalrymple thought that Wellesley, who commanded the largest fraction of the combined army, was in a position of extreme danger, yet Sir Hew contented himself with sending him a civil message from offshore and set off to cruise in search of Burrard of whose whereabouts he had no idea. There is no evidence to suggest that Sir Hew lacked physical courage but at this moment it seems that he believed that Wellesley had rashly got himself into a mess and that he, Sir Hew, was not going to get involved in it.

At one o'clock in the morning, the boat returned 'and brought advice of the action of the 21st, and also that the army had been reinforced by the brigades under Brigadier-Generals Acland and Anstruther, and that Sir Harry Burrard commanded the whole. In consequence of this intelligence my determination was immediately taken, and in the morning the frigate stood in for the shore.'[6]

128

Dalrymple, however, was not to be hurried. He spent the early part of the morning writing his letters for England and did not land until eleven o'clock. Almost the first person he met as he rode from the beach to Burrard's quarters in Maçeira village was Wellesley, who was going down to the beach to superintend the embarkation of the wounded. It was not an agreeable meeting. Dalrymple was still ruffled by Castlereagh's ill-judged letter urging him to take Sir Arthur 'into his particular confidence' and 'to make the most prominent use of him which the rules of the service will permit.' Sir Arthur, on his side, was, in all probability, in a sharp temper from Burrard's rebuff to him on the previous day. Wellesley proceeded at once 'to represent to him the necessity of an immediate advance, and stated his reasons for thinking it necessary. Sir Hew Dalrymple replied, that he had just arrived and was consequently unable to form any judgment upon the matter.'[7] Wellesley was, of course, unwise to press his views so immediately. It confirmed Dalrymple's opinion of his rashness and gave the impression, rightly, that he was trying to go behind Burrard's back. Sir Arthur remarked to his Military Secretary that 'he had to regret that it was apparent that he had not the confidence of the Commander of the Forces.'[8] Sir Hew, however, having spoken to Colonel Murray, the Quartermaster-General, sent after Wellesley confirming Burrard's preparatory orders to march on the following day.

On his way to see Sir Harry, Sir Hew gained the impression that the army was in a high state of disorganisation. He had not seen a battlefield for fifteen years and he was shaken by what he saw. A hundred and twenty carts had been unloaded and were engaged in bringing the wounded to the beach by a difficult track and every available house had been taken over to house the English and French wounded. Conditions inside these improvised hospitals were appalling. A doctor described a farm house 'whose interior was crowded with wounded. Around lay a number of poor fellows in the greatest agony, not only from the anguish of their wounds (many of which were deplorable) but from the intense heat of the sun, which increased the

parching fever induced by pain and loss of blood. Two fig trees
afforded the scanty blessing of some sort of shade to the few
who were huddled together beneath their almost leafless
branches. . . . To several, a simple inspection of their wounds,
with a few words of consolation, or perhaps a little opium, was
all that could be recommended. Of these brave men the balls
had pierced organs connected with life; and in such cases, prudence equally forbids the rash interposition of unavailing art,
and the useless indulgence of delusive hope.'[9]

With Burrard, Sir Hew had a long conference. 'The information he communicated to me was principally concerned with
the details of the action he had witnessed, and derived from his
conversation with Sir Arthur Wellesley; to the best of my recollection he did not show me any reports, or communicate any
verbal details from the officers at the heads of the artillery or
commissary departments. . . . Sir Harry estimated the number
of the enemy in the field the previous day at 14,000 at the
utmost.. . . . [He] said that there was ammunition on shore for
another battle; with respect to the artillery, he mentioned his
observation of the difficulty with which it was moved on the
day before; but I did not at all suppose that it was from the
badness of the horses, but supposed it was from their fatigue.
I do not think he entered upon an exact detail of the provisions
actually landed. The future supplies, with the exception of fresh
meat, depended upon the victuallers, and the victuallers upon
the weather. The passage between the position and the beach was
very bad, but passable on the carriages of the country. I learned
that there was a scarcity of medical stores on shore. . . . The
men's knapsacks, and every article of equipment that could
possibly be spared, had been left in the transports, and, I understood, they were sent to Oporto.'[10]

Some time after midday Sir Arthur was invited to join the
conference but 'I do not recollect that he gave me any very new
information.'[11] The conversation turned to the army's next movement and Sir Harry reported that he had sent out warning orders
for a move from the right in the direction of Mafra on the
following morning. 'Sir Arthur strongly urged the propriety of

130

moving on the next morning and . . . dwelt on the probable inconveniences of lingering on the way.'[12]

The tactical situation was now quite different from that which had faced Burrard twenty-four hours earlier. The French army was back at Torres Vedras and was rallying behind the two battalions which Junot had summoned from Lisbon on the 20th. Although, after its defeat on 21st, it was probable that it would not attempt another attack it was more than sufficient to defend the difficult pass behind Torres Vedras. The situation, therefore, was similar to that when Sir Harry and Sir Arthur had discussed it on the *Brazen* except that the initiative was now firmly in the hands of the British. The chance of getting between the French army and Lisbon had gone for good, but the former option of marching by Mafra while another corps, preferably Moore's, went to Santarem was still open. The supply position was less good than it had been. The landing of Acland's 4,000 men had reduced the number of days' supply available on shore but, apart from three days' rations in the men's packs there was available on shore '560 bags, or 61,270 lb. of bread, 60,000 lb. of salt meat, 24 puncheons of spirits.'[13] The transport position was more difficult. 'Some disorder ensued in the park during the battle, as one of the carters was killed and three wounded; several made their escape with their oxen, others by themselves, and many were prevented. The stores which were in the carts deserted by the drivers were added to the other carts, so as to have moved if indispensable the next day.'[14] In addition 120 carts had been unloaded to assist in the transport of the wounded, leaving only 240 still loaded. The view of the senior commissariat officer, who in fact was not asked for an opinion, was that it would have been difficult to move the stores but, 'I believe possible.'[15]

Before Sir Hew decided anything, Sir Arthur had left for his quarters in Vimeiro village having invited Sir Hew to dine with him that afternoon. About one o'clock a report came in from a Portuguese staff officer that the whole French army was advancing to the attack. Sir Hew, who was still convinced that 'the enemy remained formidable and entire,' therefore asked Sir

131

Arthur 'to take up the position as the day before.'[16] Hardly, however, had Sir Hew reached Vimeiro when the alarm turned out to be caused by the arrival at the outposts of the Fiftieth of General Kellermann, bearing a flag of truce and escorted by two squadrons of cavalry. Thinking that Wellesley was still in command he asked to speak to him.

Junot's view of the state of the French army coincided with Wellesley's. It was not fit to fight another battle. Its losses at Vimeiro had been heavy. It had lost some 2,000 men apart from stragglers who continued to come in for some days. It had only nine guns and the troops were demoralised by an unlooked-for defeat. The rear guard had only reached Torres Vedras at two o'clock in the morning after more than twenty-four hours of continuous marching and fighting. Exaggerated rumours were circulating about both supposed British reinforcements coming from the sea and columns of Portuguese troops moving on Santarem. Torres Vedras was defensible with the army in its present state but it was impossible to move sufficient troops across to the Mafra road to stop the British turning their flank. The alternatives facing the army were, therefore, to fall back and cover Lisbon on the line Mafra-Montechique or to abandon Lisbon, cross the Tagus into Alemtejo, march for Elvas and try to rejoin the French armies in Spain, which according to the latest of their scanty information were not likely to be met closer than Burgos. A council of war, held by Junot on the morning of 22nd August rejected both these alternatives. There only remained the possibility of a capitulation under the most favourable terms that could be obtained. This course was agreed unanimously and General Kellermann was dispatched to the British lines to drive the best bargain that he could. As he rode out from Torres Vedras, he remarked to a French officer *'qu'il allait trouver les Anglais, pour voir à nous tirer de la sourcière.'*[17]

When Wellesley heard that Kellerman had asked to speak to him, he turned to Dalrymple and 'asked him whether I should go up to the outposts and speak to General Kellermann; his answer was no; that the general had desired to speak to him, the commander-in-chief of the army, and that he would receive him at my quarters.'[18]

About two-thirty Kellermann reached Vimeiro village. An officer who was watching noted in his diary that 'Kellermann is hideously ugly, but his countenance is by no means void of *sensible* expression. He appears not to be a man of engaging address. He was accompanied by two aides-de-camp.'[19] He was received by Dalrymple alone but shortly afterwards Sir Hew asked Burrard and Wellesley to join them. He then asked Kellermann to repeat his proposals, which he did, 'reading from a paper of the wishes of the French commander-in-chief.'[20]

Kellermann's proposal was that there should be an immediate suspension of hostilities leading to a convention whereby the French should evacuate Portugal, handing over the fortresses intact. Instead of becoming prisoners of war, the French army, with 'their military baggage and equipments', should be returned to French ports in British ships. The Russian squadron should be treated as if it was in a neutral port and should be able to leave at will without interference from the Royal Navy.

The paper from which Kellermann was reading was, in fact, the draft of a definitive convention and represented the best terms that the French could, in their optimistic moments, hope to obtain. He tried to hand the paper to Wellesley, who refused to accept it. The three British generals then withdrew to another room to consider their reply.

It was clear from the start of the negotiations, even to Kellermann, that Sir Hew was delighted at the prospect of getting the French out of Portugal without further fighting. Wellesley disagreed. He wished to confine the immediate discussions to 'granting a suspension of hostilities for forty-eight hours, for the purpose of negotiating a convention for the evacuation of Portugal. . . . I told Sir Hew, that I thought there was an objection in point of form to allow the negotiation then going forward to extend to other objects than the mere suspension of hostilities; and for that reason I had declined to take the paper which he had read to us. . . . [Sir Hew] was of opinion, however, that as long as we agreed on the material point, viz. that the French

133

should be allowed to evacuate Portugal by sea, it was useless "to drive them to the wall upon a point of form" and in this manner the objection was overruled.'[21]

On the 'material point' Sir Arthur did agree with Sir Hew. The opportunity of destroying the French army had vanished the previous day owing to Sir Harry's timidity. It was not likely that Sir Hew would agree to the plan of sending a substantial body of troops, preferably Moore's corps, to Santarem to cut off the French retreat. As matters stood, an immediate French evacuation was the best outcome that could be looked for. 'The French had not only the capital, but they had Badajoz, Elvas, Almeida, and Santarem – all places that would have required sieges, as also Peniche and the Forts of St. Julian and Cascais, without the possession of which our ships could not enter the Tagus; the season of bad weather was fast approaching, and these places must have been regularly invested; and on the whole, the entire evacuation of the forts, the strong places, the capital, and the kingdom was all that the most sanguine could have desired.'[22]

On the other hand, Wellesley disagreed with some of the details of the armistice and draft convention. The two most important points were the duration of the cease fire and the position of the Russian squadron. Kellermann had proposed that the 'suspension should be unlimited in the first instance, followed by a limited suspension of forty-eight hours when either party should wish to put an end to it.' Wellesley disagreed 'in a view to the state of the resources, to the state of the season, and to the tone in which the convention was to be negotiated. . . . If we derived any advantage, I was sure that we could always prolong it.'[23] Sir Hew sided with Kellermann and decided on an unlimited armistice, although later, when the French were prolonging the negotiations for a convention, he revised his opinion and insisted on a forty-eight-hour limit.

Wellesley's other main objection was to the French attempt to include the Russian naval squadron in the evacuation agreement. 'I told [Dalrymple] what had passed between Admiral Sir Charles Cotton and me, upon this subject, in a conference

134

which I had had with the Admiral when I was at the mouth of the Tagus on the 26th and 27th of July. The Admiral had then told me, that he had heard that the Russian admiral had intended to remain neutral in the contest between British and French troops; and would claim the neutrality of the port of Lisbon; and Sir Charles asked me what I thought upon that claim. I told him that the only way of getting rid of it was to be so quick in our operations, that there would be no time for the Portuguese to make it [the claim to the neutrality of Lisbon to the Russians], before he would attack the Russian fleet; and that it was a subject upon which it would be necessary to make a reference to England. I pointed out to Sir Hew, however, that this was a claim which might be made by the Russians on their own account, or by the Portuguese in favour of the Russians, but not by the French.'[24]

There were two possibilities here. Either the Russians should be permitted to sail home unmolested or they should be allowed to stay in the estuary of the Tagus without being attacked by Cotton's squadron. Sir Hew realised that the first, which Kellermann had proposed, would be unacceptable to the Royal Navy who could not afford to have these hostile warships at large. He was, despite Wellesley's advice, prepared to agree to recognise the neutrality of Lisbon. He had, as he very well knew, no right to stipulate for the Russian fleet, this being the prerogative of the admiral. This, however, he was not prepared to admit to Kellermann, relying on Cotton to disallow the article at a later date.

Having completed their private conference, the British generals rejoined Kellermann with whom they discussed the details of the armistice, with a break for dinner, until nine o'clock at night. The conversation was in French, although Kellermann understood English and spoke it after a fashion. In this way he gained the impression that the English were far less confident of their situation than he had expected and that their expected reinforcements had not yet arrived. He gained, too, an insight into their dependence on their contact with the victualling ships when Captain Douglas, a Deputy Assistant-Quartermaster-General, 'rushed into the room, and to Sir Hew's infinite annoyance, exclaimed, very *mal à propos*, "I have been looking out for the last two hours, and the fleet is nowhere in sight." '[25] The Frenchman stiffened his terms accordingly.

According to Dalrymple, all three British generals took a full part in the discussions. 'All and each of us seemed to offer what observations we thought proper, but Sir Arthur Wellesley appeared to me to bear the prominent part in the discussion, which the situation he so lately filled, the victory he had so recently gained, and his own more perfect information upon many most important, though local, circumstances, gave him the right to assume.'[26] This was not the case. Sir Arthur had, since his first meeting with Dalrymple that morning, the impression that he had not Sir Hew's confidence. Furthermore every proposal he had made privately about the cease-fire arrangments had been overruled. Being, at best, a reserved man, it seems probable that he kept silent whenever possible. It was not, however, always possible. Dalrymple was very much aware of the advantage of having a member of the government as his colleague. This was the best insurance he could have should he make a mistake. Ministers would hesitate before censuring one of their own number.

At last all the details were settled and Kellermann dictated the fair copy of the agreement. 'Before he dictated the title he asked Sir Hew Dalrymple who was to sign it, and Sir Hew said himself. General Kellermann then represented that he, Sir Hew, ought not to sign an agreement with an inferior officer, and proposed that I [Wellesley] should sign it. Sir Hew then came into another room, where I was, and told me that General Kellermann had proposed that I should sign the instrument, and he asked me whether I had any objection to doing so. My answer was that I would sign any paper he wished me to sign. When it was drawn up, I read it over, and at the table gave it to Sir Hew Dalrymple to read, with an observation that it was a very extraordinary paper. He answered that it did not contain anything that had not been settled, and I then signed it.'[27]

The document in its final form read:

136

Cease Fire resolved between Sir Arthur Wellesley, Lieutenant-General and Knight of the Order of the Bath, and Lieutenant-General Kellermann, Grand Officer of the Legion of Honour, Commander of the Order of the Iron Crown, Grand Cross of the Order of the Lion of Bavaria: both officers having been empowered to negotiate by the Generals of the respective armies.

Headquarters of the English Army.
22nd August 1808.

Article 1. From today there will be a cease-fire between the armies of His Britannic Majesty and of His Imperial and Royal Majesty, Napoleon I, so that a Convention for the evacuation of Portugal by the French army may be negotiated.

Article 2. The Generals commanding the two armies and the Admiral commanding the British fleet at the mouth of the Tagus will meet at a time and place to be agreed in order to negotiate and conclude the said Convention.

Article 3. The River Zizandre will be established as the line of demarcation between the two armies; Neither army will occupy Torres Vedras.

Article 4. The commanding General of the English army will inform the Portuguese who are under arms of this cease-fire; and for them the line of demarcation will be established from Leiria to Tomar.

Article 5. It is provisionally agreed that in no case will the French army be considered as prisoners of war, that all members of it will be transported to France with their arms and baggage, with their personal property of every kind, nothing having been abstracted from it.

Article 6. No proceedings shall be instituted against any person, be they Portuguese, French or of a nation allied to France on the grounds of their political conduct; such people will be protected, as will be their property, and they will be at liberty to leave Portugal during a period to be agreed upon, together with their belongings.

Article 7. The port of Lisbon will be recognised as neutral as regards the Russian fleet; that is to say that while the town

137

and port are in the possession of the English, the said Russian fleet will not be molested during its stay, nor will it be stopped when it wishes to leave, nor will it be pursued after it has left until after the delay recognised by Maritime Law.

Article 8. All French artillery, as well as the horses of the cavalry, will be transported to France.

Article 9. This Cease-Fire can only be broken by giving forty-eight hours' notice.

Done and agreed by the undersigned generals at the place and time stated above.

ARTHUR WELLESLEY

KELLERMANN, *Lieutenant-General*

Additional Article. The garrisons of the fortresses occupied by the French forces will be included in the present Convention, should they not have surrendered before 25th instant.

ARTHUR WELLESLEY

KELLERMANN, *Lieutenant-General*.[28]

As Wellesley had said, it was 'a very extraordinary paper.' It was, without doubt, a personal triumph for Kellermann. That morning the French generals had considered the position of their army to be hopeless. Kellermann's skill in negotiation had made it possible for it to return to France, if not with honour, at least as a complete fighting formation. There was not even the stipulation, common in those days, that the troops should not fight again in the Peninsula. In fact the whole corps was back in Spain before the end of the year and twelve out of Junot's twenty-two regular battalions* returned to Portugal with Marshal Masséna when in 1810 he swept up to the Lines of Torres Vedras. Some of them (e.g. 2me Léger and 70me Ligne) were still in line against the British when Wellington forced his way over the Pyrenees in 1813.

On Dalrymple's side it was a masterpiece of ineptitude. Every article could be objected to on political or military grounds. Even the first article, a straightforward declaration of intention to

---

* Junot had, in addition to his regular battalions, two provisional battalions made up of drafts and detachments.

138

negotiate, referred to Napoleon as *'sa Majesté Imperiale et Royale'*, a dignity which the British had steadfastly refused to admit. Articles 4, 6 and the additional article were grossly offensive to the Portuguese, firstly because Dalrymple undertook to regulate the movements of the Portuguese army and to re-patriate prisoners taken by them after 25th August although he had no command in the Portuguese army, and, secondly, because he undertook that there should be no reprisals against Portu-guese traitors, an undertaking which only a Portuguese civil government could give.

Articles 2 and 7 set out to bind the Royal Navy both to treat with the French army and to let the Russian fleet go free. Both were immediately repudiated by Admiral Cotton.

Article 3 left all the defensible positions in French hands while Article 9 gave the French every possible chance of fortifying them should the negotiations break down at a later stage. Article 8 was, perhaps, the least harmful but, by agreeing to permit the French to take away their horses, it deprived the British of the one spoil of war which would have been of the greatest value to them. Never has a victorious army with every advantage in its hands signed an agreement which gave so much to its defeated enemies with so little to itself.

Colonel Torrens recalled that 'at daylight on the morning of the 23rd, Sir Arthur Wellesley mentioned to me the occurrences which had taken place the evening before; and mentioned that he had signed the armistice by the desire of Sir Hew Dalrymple, although he totally disapproved of many points in it, and of the tone of the language in which it was drawn up.'[29]

References

Chapter 7. *'A Very Extraordinary Paper'*

1 Cintra 63. Evidence of HD
2 ib
3 ib
4 ib 66

5   ib 65
6   ib
7   Cintra 116. Evidence of Torrens
8   ib
9   Neale: letter of 22 Aug '08
10 Cintra 119. Evidence of HD
11 ib
12 ib
13 Cintra 90. Evidence of Deputy Commissary General Pippon
14 ib
15 ib
16 HD 63
17 Hulot, q. in Oman i 267
18 Cintra 100. Evidence of AW
19 Neale 53
20 Cintra 100. Evidence of AW
21 Cintra 101–2. Evidence of AW
22 Croker ii 122
23 Cintra 103–4. Evidence of AW
24 ib 102
25 Colborne 85
26 Cintra 19. Evidence of HD
27 Cintra 104. Evidence of AW
28 Cintra 1–2
29 Cintra 116. Evidence of Torrens

CHAPTER 8

'My Situation is a Very

F ROM the moment that he signed it, Wellesley realised that his signature on the armistice laid him open to attack. Dalrymple's request to him to sign it had put him into an intolerable position. Having known Sir Hew for only a few hours and already being on bad terms with him, to refuse might seem an act of open disaffection and one that could certainly not be kept from the army who were already showing signs of resentment against those who had superseded their victorious commander and who, they felt, had robbed them of the fruits of victory. He felt, therefore, that he could not properly decline. Instead he steadfastly maintained that he was not responsible. 'If the Commander of the Forces had given me instructions to negotiate this instrument, and had I then negotiated it, I might have been responsible for its contents; or at all events for the manner in which it was drawn up; but as it is, my signature is a mere form.'[1]

On the day after the agreement was signed he wrote a long private letter to Castlereagh. 'Although my name is affixed to this instrument, I beg that you will not believe that I negotiated it, that I approve of it, or that I had any hand in wording it. It was negotiated by the General himself in my presence and that

Delicate One'

of Sir Harry Burrard; and after it had been drawn out by
Kellermann himself, Sir Hew Dalrymple desired me to sign it.
I object to its *verbiage*; I object to an indefinite suspension of
hostilities; it ought to have been forty-eight hours only. As it
is now, the French will have forty-eight hours to prepare for
their defence, after Sir Hew will put an end to the suspension.'

'I approve of allowing the French to evacuate Portgual, more
particularly as it appears to be deemed impossible to move Sir
John Moore's corps to Santarem, so as to cut off the retreat
of the French towards Elvas. They could establish themselves
in Elvas, Fort La Lippe, Almeida and Peniche, which places we
should be obliged either to blockade or attack regularly in the
worst season of the year . . . and the advance of the army into
Spain would be delayed. It is more to the advantage of the
general cause to have 30,000 Englishmen in Spain and 10,000
or 12,000 additional Frenchmen on the northern frontier of Spain,
than to have Frenchmen in Portugal, and the Englishmen
employed in the blockade or siege of strong places. If they are
to be allowed to evacuate it must be with their property; but
I should have wished to adopt some method of making the

143

French generals disgorge the church plate which they have stolen.

'I will not conceal from you, my dear Lord, that my situation in this army is a very delicate one. I never saw Sir Hew Dalrymple till yesterday; and it is not an easy task to advise any man on the first day one meets with him. He must at least be prepared to receive advice. Then I have been very successful with the army, and they don't appear to me to like to go to anybody else for orders or instructions upon any subject. This is another awkward circumstance which cannot end well; and to tell you the truth, I should prefer going home to staying here. However, if you wish me to stay I will: I only beg that you will not blame me if things should not go on as you and my friends in London might wish they should.'[2]

A few days later he wrote to another friend 'I have only to regret that I signed the agreement for a suspension of hostilities without having negotiated. I have already told you the reasons why I did so, but I doubt whether good nature, and a deference to the opinion of an officer appointed Commander-in-Chief on the day of his taking his command, and to his orders, and a desire to avoid being considered the head of a party against his authority, will be deemed sufficient excuses for an act which, on the other grounds, I cannot justify.'[3] Meanwhile, not being a man to repine, he wrote, on 23rd August, to Captain Malcolm of the *Donegal* that 'I shall be much obliged to you if you will have another cask of my claret broken up and put in chests such as the last.'[4]

On that day the army, at last, moved forward and, according to the Armistice, took up the line of the Zizandre, Dalrymple moving his headquarters to Ramalhal, and the army camping around the town except for Craufurd's brigade which was left to guard the beach-head at Maçeira. Colonel Murray was dispatched, through the French lines, to Lisbon from where he was to communicate the terms of the cease-fire to Admiral Cotton. Hardly had Sir Hew settled into his new abode than he was visited by General Bernardino Freire. The Portuguese general was, not unnaturally, angry. He had heard of the agree-

144

ment, of which Sir Hew had not sent him a copy, and disapproved of what he had heard. For the moment he was pacified by being given a copy and Dalrymple's promise to receive a liaison officer to represent the Portuguese objections. Freire took his leave but very shortly afterwards, the liaison officer, Major Ayres Pinto de Souza, took his place.

Pinto de Souza took the greatest objection to Article 6 'which undertook for the protection of certain obnoxious persons, whose fate, he observed, must ultimately depend upon the government of the country.'⁵ Sir Hew defended himself on the only ground which was even slightly tenable – that no effective government existed in Portugal. The Regency left behind by Prince Regent John was suspected, with much reason, of having collaborated with the French and was, consequently, unacceptable until it was reconstituted. Souza did not go as far as to claim that the Junta of Oporto, under whom Freire served, should be recognised as the future government yet 'he seemed to insinuate that all Portugal not under the dominion of the French, already acknowledged the provisional power of the Junta of Oporto, he yet, upon my observing that I knew of another provincial government in the province of Algarve, admitted that to be the case, but with the explanation, that Algarve was not considered a part of Portugal, but a separate province annexed thereto.'⁶ Dalrymple, thereupon, told Souza to ask Freire to put his objections into writing and thus closed the interview. Freire did not do so. Instead, he informed the Junta of the situation. They, in their turn, complained over Dalrymple's head to London.

Late on the 24th August Murray returned to Ramalhal with a verbal message from the Admiral that he could not agree to the Russians being included in the armistice, but that he would open purely naval negotiations with Admiral Siniavin. Cotton was, however, prepared to be associated with Dalrymple in the military discussions with Junot. Sir Hew, therefore, wrote a letter to the French general telling him of Cotton's decision but softening it by adding 'I feel myself however fully authorised to assure your Excellency, that the objection on the part of the British Admiral does not proceed from any desire to push to the utmost the advantages which the actual state of the war in this quarter might present to the British forces.'[7] Murray, thereupon, set out once more to Lisbon armed not only with this letter to Junot but with authority to treat on the basis of the remaining articles.

Murray's authority to treat was hedged around with conditions. In the intervening three days Dalrymple seems to have come to the belated conclusion that Wellesley had given him the right advice in the earlier negotiations. Moreover, on 24th August, Sir John Moore landed at Maçeira and the first of his troops were close behind him. The British military position would, in the next few days, become so overwhelmingly strong that even Dalrymple and Burrard need have no fears about further operations. Thus, in the letter authorising Murray to negotiate, the first paragraph stated that 'as it is exceedingly inconvenient and disadvantageous to the British Army to be liable to the agreement for an unlimited Suspension of Hostilities, you will inform His Excellency that I shall consider that to which I have agreed to be at an end at 12 o'clock at noon on the 28th.'[8]

There was also a memorandum, drawn up by Wellesley, which was intended to put as many teeth as possible into the Armistice agreement. Firm dates were to be set for the handing over of all the Portuguese fortresses and the British were to have the 'use of the port of Lisbon, and the navigation of the Tagus' from the moment that the definitive convention was signed. Details of the method of transporting the French army were to be fixed, not only the mode of paying for the hire, but security for their return 'as fifty of those sent with the army of Egypt were detained in France.'* The French were to be taken to Rochefort as 'being the greatest distance from Spain and the Austrian frontier.'† The agreement to repatriate the French horses was to be rescinded. So few were the British cavalry that any available horse-

---

* In 1801, after the battle of Alexandria and the capture of Cairo, a very similar convention was entered into for the return of the French army to France in British ships.
† War between France and Austria did not break out until April of the following year but already Britain was looking to Austria as a future ally.

transports were urgently needed to bring out reinforcements. The French, instead, were permitted to attempt to hire horse transports, which was probably impossible, or to sell them in Lisbon. There were two other points to be attended to. First, there was to be an exchange of prisoners, an obvious necessity which had been overlooked in the Armistice; secondly: 'Some mode to be devised to make the French generals disgorge the church plate which they have stolen.'[9]

Murray and Kellerman started discussions in Lisbon on the morning of 26th August and, for a time, all went well despite a proposal from the French that they should be permitted to remove the *Vasco de Gama*, a Portuguese ship of the line, and several Portuguese frigates which had not been ready for sea when the Portuguese fleet sailed for the Brazils in 1807. The French, having refitted them, now claimed them as legitimate spoil of war and hoped to carry them away. Murray firmly declined.

While Murray was riding to and fro between Lisbon and Ramalhal, Moore had landed at Maçeira, where he heard the first news of the victory at Vimeiro and the Armistice. His first impression of the state of the army was very unfavourable. In his diary he wrote: 'I am sorry to find everything in the greatest confusion, and a very general discontent. Sir Hew, though announced to the army, had not as yet taken the direction of it; much was still done by Sir Arthur Wellesley, and what was not done by him was not done at all. The action on the 21st had been very complete. . . . Sir Arthur's wish was to have followed them, in which case I believe he would have been in Lisbon next day; but Sir Harry Burrard would not allow him. He had in the same manner been prevented by Sir Harry Burrard from attacking the French the day before. . . . Sir Arthur's views on both occasions were extremely right. . . . It is evident that if any operation is to be carried on it will be miserably conducted, and that seniority in the Army List is a bad guide in the choice of a military commander. Sir Arthur Wellesley seems to have conducted his operations with ability, and they have been crowned with success. It is a pity, when so much has been thrown in his hands, that he has not been allowed to complete it, and the conduct of the government on this occasion has been absurd to a degree.'[10] He lost no time in writing to congratulate Wellesley, whom he had never met, and received by return a friendly letter, assuring him that 'nothing could have given me greater pleasure than to have assisted you in the performance of the services which my good fortune has allotted to me. At all events I wish that you had arrived a few days sooner, that you might by your influence have prevailed with those who prevented me from making all the use in my power of the victory which the troops had gained. But you are not now too late, and I hope that you will soon come to headquarters and ascertain the state and means of this army, and state your opinion respecting the means to be adopted. . . . In less than a fortnight it will not be possible for a fleet to remain on the coast of Portugal, excepting in Lisbon or Oporto. About that time the rains will begin to fall, the troops must have tents, and the roads will become more difficult than they are at present. All these circumstances appear to have been forgotten, and we have done nothing since the 21st. I am therefore very desirous indeed that you should come over here, and I assure you that you will find our situation to be well deserving of your serious consideration, and the exercise of your influence for the purpose of setting us right.'[11]

On the evening of 25th August Moore reached Ramalhal and saw Sir Hew. He formed no high opinion of him, describing him as 'a man certainly not without sense, but who had never before served in the field as a general officer, who had allowed a war of sixteen years to pass without pushing for any service except in England and Guernsey, and who seemed to be completely at a loss in the situation in which he was placed.'[12] He made it plain to Sir Hew that, in his opinion, Wellesley had been right in his judgment and Sir Hew and Sir Harry wrong. 'I have told both Sir Hew and Sir Arthur that I wished not to interfere; that if the hostilities commenced, Sir Arthur had already done so much, that I thought it but fair he should have the command of whatever was brilliant in the finishing. I waived all pretensions as senior. I considered this as his expedition. He should have the command of whatever was detached. For my part I wished I could withdraw myself altogether; but I should aid as far as I could for the good of the service, and without interference with Sir Arthur, I should take any part that was allotted to me.'[13]

Moore's corps, which included a regiment of light dragoons nearly 600 strong, continued to land until the 29th. The surf on the beach, always a hazard, was rising steadily. Disembarkation in the flat-bottomed boats became a dangerous business. 'The men sat four by four on the thwarts, all pressed closely together, with their packs and muskets between their legs. None of the officers was allowed to take more than a valise with him. With beating hearts we approached the first line of surf, and were lifted high up into the air. We clung frantically to our seats, and all of us had to crouch quite low. Not a few closed their eyes and prayed, but I did not close mine before we were actually in the foam of the roaring breakers on the beach. There were twenty to thirty British sailors on the beach, all quite naked who, the moment the foremost breakers withdrew, dashed like lightning into the surf, and after many vain efforts, during which they were often caught up and thrown back by the waves, at last succeeded in casting a long rope to us, which we were able to seize. Then, with a loud hurrah, they ran at top speed through the advancing breakers up the beach, dragging us with them, until the boat stuck fast, and there was only a little spray from the surf to wet us. Finally, seizing a favourable opportunity, when a retreating wave had withdrawn sufficiently far, each of them took a soldier on his back, and carried him on to the dry shore.'[14] It was obvious to all who watched, that it would not be possible to supply the army over the beaches if the weather should deteriorate further. To point the lesson, a boatload of the infantry of the German Legion was overturned and its complement lost.

Meanwhile the negotiations in Lisbon were dragging. Apart from the French claim to the Portuguese men-of-war, they put forward 'an inadmissible pretention' not to release the Spanish prisoners whom they held in hulks in the Tagus without a comparable number of French prisoners in Spain being released.

Further complications were caused by a Portuguese force which advanced beyond the cease-fire line in the direction of Santarem. After consultation with Burrard and Wellesley, but not, according to his own account, with Moore, Dalrymple modified some of his instructions to Murray and agreed to extend the cease-fire by twenty-four hours to noon on the 29th. That was as far as he would go. On the 28th a large corps under Wellesley was moved to within a short distance of the neutral zone around the town of Torres Vedras.

At six in the morning of the 29th an aide-de-camp arrived from Lisbon with a provisional convention signed by Murray and Kellermann but which required Dalrymple's ratification. He immediately called a meeting of the lieutenant-generals which was attended by Burrard, Moore, Hope, Frazer and Wellesley. Only Lord Paget was absent, his quarters being too far distant for him to be summoned in time. The meeting, for which Wellesley took the minutes, decided that some alterations must be made. A further letter was sent to Murray, further troops were brought up to the vicinity of Torres Vedras, and on the 31st, in the presence of all the lieutenant-generals except Wellesley, Dalrymple ratified the convention at his headquarters at Torres Vedras, whither he had moved them the previous day.

The final Convention followed fairly closely the lines laid down in the Armistice as modified by the instructions given to Murray. Only on one point was Murray thoroughly unsuccessful. He was forced to agree, and Sir Hew did not dispute the point, that the repatriation of the French should be not only in British ships but at British expense. The Spaniards were to be set free without exchange but Dalrymple undertook, mysteriously, 'to obtain of the Spaniards to restore such French subjects, either military or civil, as may have been detained in Spain without being taken in battle, or in consequence of military operations, but on occasion of the occurrences of the 29th May last, and the days immediately following.' It was not found possible to devise an acceptable form of words to force the French generals to disgorge their loot but commissioners were appointed and

150

the interception of French booty loomed large in the work which Major-General Beresford and Lieutenant-Colonel Lord Proby, the British Commissioners, had to do in Lisbon. The clauses about Portuguese traitors were repeated despite the protests of Freire.

The forts commanding the Tagus were surrendered immediately and all other fortresses as soon as British troops could reach them, except in Lisbon where they were to be retained until all the French had embarked. The British army was to move to within three leagues of Lisbon. There was also included a clause, normal at that time, that 'should there arise doubts as to the meaning of any article it shall be explained favourably to the French.'[15] This was harmless in itself, but gave a convenient handle to those who wished, for one reason and another, to decry the Convention.

In consequence of the ratification, troops landing from the sea took over the forts of St. Julian, Cascais and Bugio on 2nd September, thus securing the mouth of the Tagus. On the same day the main army advanced to the area Mafra – Chilieros – Cintra. Dalrymple established his headquarters at Cintra and it was from there that he wrote his first dispatch, covering the Armistice and the Convention on 3rd September. This was a cleverly worded document, which, dwelling on the fact that 'as I landed in Portugal entirely unacquainted with the actual state of the French army, and many circumstances of a local and incidental nature,' contrived, while not mentioning Wellesley's name in connection with the 'signal defeat' inflicted on the French at Vimeiro, to imply that that officer had handled completely the negotiations for cease-fire. 'A few hours after my arrival, General Kellermann came in with a flag of truce from the French general-in-chief, in order to propose an agreement for a cessation of hostilities, for the purpose of concluding a convention for the evacuation of Portugal by the French troops; though several articles, at first agreed upon, were signed by Sir Arthur Wellesley and General Kellermann, but as this was done with a reference to the British admiral, who, when the agreement was communicated to him, objected to the 7th article'[16] was the form of words he used to describe the armistice discussions. No word of it was actually untrue but to the ordinary reader the inference was clear that Sir Hew, with becoming modesty, had left the negotiations to his victorious subordinate.

*   *   *

On 3rd September the General Officers who had served under Wellesley at Vimeiro wrote to him that: 'Anxious to manifest the high esteem and respect we bear towards you, and the satisfaction we must ever feel in having had the good fortune to serve under your command, we have this day directed a piece of plate, value 1,000 guineas, to be prepared and presented to you.'[17] This was most gratifying, the more so since, three days later, 'the commanding officers of corps and field officers, who have had the honour of serving in the army under your command,' also addressed him in a similar fashion. Nevertheless, with the signing of the Convention, Sir Arthur felt that his task was done. For the Chief Secretary for Ireland to put his office into commission to command an expeditionary force, or even to hold high rank in it, was justifiable. To command a division of seven battalions at a time when there was no fighting was not. Moreover his personal position was increasingly difficult. Sir Hew made it clear that Wellesley had not got his confidence while the army he had commanded regarded him as a hero and viewed Sir Hew with barely veiled contempt.

On 5th September Wellesley wrote to Castlereagh asking permission to leave the army. 'It is quite impossible for me to continue any longer with this army; and I wish, therefore, that you would allow me to go home and resume the duties of my office, if I should still be in office, and if it is convenient to the government that I should retain it; or if not, that I should remain upon the staff in England; or, if that should not be practicable, that I should remain without employment. You will hear from others of the various causes which I must have for being dissatisfied, not only with the military and other measures of the Commander-in-Chief, but with his treatment of myself. I am

152

convinced it is better for him, for the army, and for me, that I should go away; and the sooner I go the better.'[18]

Dalrymple, at the same time, was anxious to get rid of Wellesley and needing a senior officer to go to Madrid, offered the task to Wellesley. 'I feel very much disposed to send to Madrid an officer high in military rank and family connexion; but above all, distinguished as a statesman and a soldier. . . . To hold a language that may bring these people to their senses. . . . The description being given, I need not add that I had you in view.'[19] Sir Hew knew, better than any one with the army, the difficulty of dealing with the Spaniards and it was obvious that no good was likely to come of such a mission. He received an icy reply. 'In order to be able to perform the important part allotted to him, this person should possess the confidence of those who employ him; and, above all, in order that he may recommend with authority, a plan to the Spaniards, he should be acquainted with those of his employers, the means by which they propose to carry them into execution, and those by which they intend to enable the Spanish nation to execute that which will be proposed to them. I certainly cannot consider myself as possessing those advantages.'[20]

In the meantime the French army was embarking for its voyage home, all being away by 18th September.* Their departure was the subject of much wrangling with the British commissioners. Junot had set his troops a bad example by sending back to France with the aide-de-camp, whom he had been allowed to dispatch to announce the Convention to Paris, a Bible from the Royal Library which his wife later sold for 85,000 francs. He also attempted to claim that all the horses and mules in the Royal stables were his personal property. Although most of the rest of the Royal Library and the Natural History Museum, which the French had crated ready for sailing, was intercepted nothing could be done to regain the looted church plate and the French Paymaster-General, after the Convention, removed £25,000 from the *Deposito Publico* which he placed in the military chest and embarked, having paid none of the army's

* The outlying garrisons of Elvas and Almeida followed later.

bills in Lisbon. It was only after this individual had been arrested
on board ship and brought back to Lisbon that some measure of
restitution was obtained. In the words of the British Commissioners in their final report, 'the conduct of the French has been
marked by the most shameful disregard to honour and probity,
publicly evincing their intention of carrying off their plundered
booty, and leaving acknowledged debts unpaid.'[21]

Not that the French were having an easy time. As their numbers decreased with embarkation individual Frenchmen were
murdered by the Portuguese in growing numbers. As early as
5th September, Kellermann, the French Commissioner, was
begging the British to appoint an officer with powers to maintain
order in the city. British troops had to be moved in and an
officer of the Forty-Fifth recalled how on 'the evening after our
arrival I was sent with the outlying piquet to strengthen the
main guard. I had hardly arrived when a Frenchman came running to the guard room to claim protection, and presently two
more appeared followed up by a large mob. The first arrival
was a merchant who had resided fifteen years in Lisbon; the
second was a barber, of the same period of residence; the only
one connected with the arrival of the French army was the last
of the three, who had been a waiter in a coffee house in the Rocio
square. I had the guard and piquet turned out, left room for
the fugitives to pass, and stopped the pursuers; who called out
"Viva los Ingleses", said the runaways were Frenchmen, and
expected that they would be given up directly to their vengeance.
It was in vain to argue with such persons; they kept pressing
on to the men, so that I feared they would get within our bayonet
points. I ordered three men to load with ball cartridge, and told
the mob that I would shoot anyone who endeavoured to force
his way. This had the desired effect: they drew off and broke
into groups.'[22]

The British were hardly more popular with the Portuguese than
the French. Beresford wrote from Lisbon to Wellesley that: 'The
people here of every class are enraged to the highest degree, and
this treaty has lowered us much in their estimation.'[23] Dalrymple
was besieged with further protests about his neglect of Portuguese

154

interests and matters were scarcely improved when, acting on a discretion given him by London, he appointed a new Portuguese Council of Regency. On 23rd September he paid a formal call on the new Regents. Moore, who accompanied him, thought poorly of his performance. 'The necessity for a speech on this occasion had not, I believe, occurred to Sir Hew. He had prepared none. After he had made his bow and they theirs, there was a pause. They evidently expected to be addressed, and Sir Hew was a little confused to find he had nothing to say. He, however, recovered himself, and muttered something which I could not hear. The interview was awkward enough, and we retired, returning as we had come in state carriages to General Beresford's.'[24]

Wellesley did not wait for an answer to his letter to Castlereagh before seeking Dalrymple's permission to leave for England. Having heard that Mr. Traill, his deputy in Ireland, had died, he wrote to Sir Hew on 17th September 'for leave to go to England by the first ship that shall sail.'[25] This was immediately granted. Before he left, however, he took the opportunity of having a long talk with Sir John Moore. He wrote to him on 17th September asking for an interview and setting out his views on the state of the army. 'It appears to me to be quite impossible that we can go on as we are now constituted; the Commander-in-Chief must be changed, and the country and the army naturally turn their eyes to you as their commander.'[26] It was a remarkable, almost mutinous, letter for an officer to write to his senior about their chief, but Wellesley justified it by considering himself in his political capacity, as a member of the ministry, rather than as a soldier. He saw that Moore was the only man who could make a success of the coming campaign and wished to offer his good offices with the cabinet in London. 'I understand that you have lately had some unpleasant discussions with the King's ministers, the effect of which might be to prevent the adoption of an arrangement for the command of this army which in my opinion would be the best, and would enable you to render those services at this moment for which you are peculiarly qualified. I wish you would allow me to talk

155

to you respecting the discussions to which I have adverted, in order that I may endeavour to remove any trace which they may have left on the minds of the King's ministers, having the effect which I have supposed.

'Although I hold high office under Government, I am no party man, but have long been connected in friendship with many of those persons who are now at the head of affairs in England; and I think I have sufficient influence over them, that they may listen to me upon a point of this description, more particularly as I am convinced that they must be as desirous as I can be to adopt the arrangement for the command of this army which all are agreed is the best.'[27]

Moore was surprised and, perhaps, a little shocked by this approach but agreed to see Wellesley. 'I told him that with respect to our present commander I might think of him as he did; it was impossible not to see how unfit he was for the station in which he was placed, and not to regret that he was ever named to it. But it was the business of Government to remove him if they thought proper. I could enter into no intrigue upon the subject.'[28] Nevertheless, he told him at length about his ill-treatment at the hands of the cabinet and of 'my wish . . . to remove any impression which should prevent me from being employed, and I would be obliged to him or any other friend who would be kind enough to do it, . . . [although] I would not, for the sake of any situation, make a submission, or anything that tended to it, which I thought unbecoming.'[29]

The two men parted as friends, Sir Arthur having Sir John's permission 'to state to Lord Castlereagh that I had explained candidly my feelings, that I had no ill-will to Lord Castlereagh or to any of the Administration; they had been wanting to me, and I had told them so and there with me it ended.'[30] In fact, there was no need for Sir Arthur's good offices. Before he reached England ministers had come to his conclusions before he could offer his advice.

On 21st September Wellesley with his staff boarded H.M.S. *Plover*, sloop of war, in the Tagus and set out for England. The doctor already quoted wrote home: 'The departure of Sir Arthur

Wellesley for England is a subject of great regret with the army. He had won the entire confidence and affections of the soldiery, in an uncommon degree, by his talents and affability.'[31]

References

Chapter 8. 'My situation is a very delicate one'

1 Cintra 106. Evidence of AW
2 SD vi 124. AW to Castlereagh, 23 Aug '08
3 SD vi 132. AW to Richmond, 9 Sept '08
4 WD iv 118. AW to Malcolm, 23 Aug '08
5 Cintra 71. Evidence of HD
6 ib
7 Cintra 346. HD to Junot, 25 Aug '08
8 Cintra 344. HD to Murray, 25 Aug '08
9 ib
10 Moore Diary ii 257–58
11 ib 256
12 ib 259
13 ib 258–59
14 Schaumann 1–2
15 Cintra 5
16 Cintra 328. HD to Castlereagh, 3 Sept '08
17 WD iv 137
18 WD iv 147. AW to Castlereagh, 5 Sept '08
19 SD vi 134. HD to AW, 9 Sept '08
20 WD iv 152–53. AW to HD, 10 Sept '08
21 Cintra 414. Beresford and Proby to HD, 18 Sept '08
22 PS i 16. Wilkie
23 SD vi 129. Beresford to AW, 5 Sept '08
24 Moore Diary ii 267
25 WD iv 159. AW to HD, 17 Sept '08
26 WD iv 156. AW to Moore, 17 Sept '08
27 ib
28 Moore Diary ii 265
29 ib
30 ib
31 Neale, 6 Oct '08

'This Dishonourable and

I N the early nineteenth century, when communications were slow and unsure and newspapers did not employ regular foreign correspondents,* the Press was forced to rely for overseas news on such public dispatches as ministers saw fit to release, augmented by such rumours as could be collected from sea-captains, merchants and other travellers. They, therefore, spent much of their space denying such incorrect information as their competitors, and even themselves had previously published. Thus, while Wellesley's force was sailing to Portugal from Cork, most of the news from the Peninsula consisted of imaginary reports of French defeats in Spain, Dupont being the most frequent victim, until the true account of his surrender at Bailen on 19th July made the headlines on 9th August. Meanwhile there was on 21st July a story, wholly without foundation, that Marshal Bessières was marching into Portugal to Junot's aid. The Marshal was marching towards the province of Biscay in exactly the opposite direction at that time but this could not be

---

* *The Times* had sent out Henry Crabb Robinson to Spain in July 1808. He, however, never got beyond Coruña, where, in the following January, he was able to obtain a remarkable scoop.

158

'Unprecedented Transaction'

known in London. On the same day it was reported from Portugal that General Loison had captured two regiments of Portuguese regulars and London would have been very alarmed had it been known that in the whole of Portugal there were not two regiments of regular Portuguese troops.

Reports of Wellesley's progress were no more accurate. On 8th August a rumour was current that he had landed at Mondego Bay but on the following day the *Morning Chronicle* stated: 'Information was received yesterday of the landing of Sir Arthur Wellesley with all his force. The landing did not take place at Figueira, as was generally expected, but at Peniche, which is nearer to Lisbon. The debarkation was completed by the 30th ult; and when these accounts came away, Sir Arthur's advanced-guard had reached Mafra, which is within 26 miles of Lisbon. Important, and we hope grateful, news may be hourly expected from this quarter.'

Since this item had landed the army seventy miles and nine days nearer the enemy than actually occurred, it was hardly surprising that the 'important and grateful news' was not forth-coming and three days later, on 12th August, the same paper was reduced to correcting its rivals' errors. 'It was universally

159

reported yesterday afternoon, that an account had been received by Ministers of the surrender of Junot to Sir Arthur Wellesley – but we can assure our readers that no such advice was received, either by courier or telegraph. We are confident that the event will happen, for the surrender of Dupont and the retreat of Bessières must deprive him of all hope of succour. As soon, therefore, as the army of Sir Arthur Wellesley shall be sufficiently advanced to protect him from the revenge which his conduct may give him reason to apprehend from the Portuguese, we hope he will surrender without bloodshed. By that means our fine army would be kept entire for immediate service. Care, however, must be taken that he shall not be allowed to secrete and withdraw his ill-gotten booty.' The paper had rightly weighed up Junot's predatory habits if not his military determination.

News of the real landing arrived in time for the papers of 16th August. The *Chronicle* reported: 'Yesterday Mr. Basilico, the messenger, arrived in the *Encounter* gun-brig, with dispatches from Sir Arthur Wellesley. He brings an account that on the 1st instant Sir Arthur began to land his army at Figueiras; on the 3rd they were all disembarked.' So far the report was correct but the paper went on, 'a report was current that General Spencer had landed his force at St. Ube's [Setubal], but we think this is doubtful. . . . If it be true, it must be in consequence of an understanding with Sir Arthur, and of accurate knowledge of Junot's position. A ministerial paper of last night says that the two armies have formed a junction; but this is obviously inconsistent with the report of their having landed at such a distance from one another, and in two opposite points. As to the possibility of Junot's surrender without a battle, no man can speak with any thing like reason. . . . It would appear to be his most sensible proceeding to capitulate, as it would be Sir Arthur Wellesley's policy to accept it, and to grant him easy terms. His position is so strong that he might hold out for a long time, and it is for the interests of the allies that our army should be speedily released from this service, that it may proceed on another.

160

'We are gratified to read in Admiral Cotton's proclamation that Junot's army does not amount to more than 10,000 men.'

Newspapers have short memories. It will surprise no one that the same paper, within a month, was describing the 'easy terms' supposedly granted to Junot by Wellesley as 'scandalously disgraceful'.

After this, news from Portugal dried up. On the 23rd the idea of Spencer having landed apart from the main body was still believed though in a different form. On the 23rd it was reported that 'General Spencer landed at a point more southerly than Sir Arthur Wellesley: he landed at Mafra. General Anstruther also landed, but it was not till the 12th.' Into this dearth of news, however, there came a report of an undoubted success – the publication of dispatches from Rear-Admiral Keats, commanding in the Baltic, who told how the Royal Navy had, after elaborate secret negotiations, rescued from the Danish islands the Spanish general, the Marquis de la Romaña, and a corps of 6,000 troops who had been forced to serve under French command. This true, Hornblower-like coup, occupied the news columns for some days during a dull patch and as late as 30th August, all that could be said about the army was that 'the reports from Portugal are not important. They come down only to the 9th inst. Junot remains in his positions, and Sir Arthur Wellesley was on his march; but it is the universal opinion that he will display a truly wise and dignified forebearance, by not making the attack until the arrival of the army of Sir Harry Burrard.'

The news broke on 2nd September. On that day the *Chronicle* announced: 'We have great joy in communicating to the public the following most important and glorious intelligence: Major Campbell (aide-de-camp to Sir Arthur Wellesley) arrived yesterday evening with dispatches from Lieutenant-General Sir Arthur Wellesley.' The news he brought covered both Roliça and Vimeiro, both of which were announced as major victories, a title which Roliça certainly did not deserve. It was further reported that 'Sir Harry Burrard himself arrived in the course of the action [Vimeiro] but did not take command of the army. He left Sir Arthur Wellesley to fight out the battle. . . . General Junot had on the 23rd offered to capitulate; but he had not surrendered when Major Campbell came away.' This last piece of news was a piece of wishful thinking. According to Mr. Ross, Private Secretary to Canning, all that was known was that 'General Kellermann had sent in a flag of truce just before Colonel Browne* came away; he is ignorant of its precise object.'[1] That a subordinate general had sent in a flag of truce need not have meant anything. Flags of truce were very common in those days and the fact that General Brennier was a prisoner in British hands would have meant that the French would certainly have sent across to the British with his baggage and some money. The Press and public, however, had convinced themselves that Junot's position was hopeless, even before his defeat, and that his only course would be to surrender.

The truth was that Britain, not having won a significant land battle since Alexandria seven years before, was yearning for a victory. Ministers, too, needed a triumph and did everything they could to build up Vimeiro in the public mind. On receiving the dispatches, Castlereagh wrote a public letter to the Lord Mayor saying that 'It is impossible to speak of the victory obtained by Sir Arthur Wellesley in terms and exultation too high, for certainly it is an event not less splendid in gallantry than it is important in its results. It has demonstrated a truth which it was most essential to verify, that our troops only require to be well conducted to display their excellence.'[2] The Tower guns were fired.

The actual dispatches were not published in the newspapers until after the weekend and in the meantime public expectation was raised still further by news from less official sources. At 1 p.m. on Saturday, 3rd September, the following notice was posted at Lloyds. 'A gentleman of this house has just received a letter from Oporto, dated the 28th last, which states that Junot

* Colonel Browne, an officer sent by the government on a special mission to Portugal, returned on the same ship as Major Campbell.

162

with his army had decamped from Lisbon, to which he had retreated after the defeat of the 21st, and was attacked on the 24th by the British army; that General Loison and 5,000 were killed in the action, and that Junot and the remainder were made prisoners. Thirty-three waggons, loaded with plate and other valuables, of which the French had plundered the City of Lisbon, fell into the hands of the British army. The Russian fleet in the Tagus had hoisted Portuguese colours.'[3]

This optimistic Portuguese invention appeared in the London papers on Monday 5th September, together with Burrard's dispatch to Castlereagh of 21st August which was little more than a short covering letter to Wellesley's report to him. In neither document was any hint given of any disagreement between the generals. Wellesley had not mentioned the lost possibility of pursuing the routed French and Burrard paid a most handsome compliment to Wellesley. 'I was fortunate enough to reach the field of action in time to witness and approve of every disposition that had been made, and was afterwards made by Sir Arthur Wellesley; his comprehensive mind furnishing a ready resource in every emergency, and rendering it quite unnecessary to direct any alteration.'[4]

Editorial comment was lyrical about the battle but critical of the way the army had been equipped. 'One cannot read Sir Arthur Wellesley's accounts of the two engagements of the British troops, without admiring the perspicuity and precision with which they are drawn up, as well as the skill of his arrangements as a general. . . . The position of the army when it was attacked by the French at Vimeiro, reflects the greatest credit upon the talents of its gallant and most distinguished leader. . . . Sir Arthur, it will be observed, repeatedly complains of the disadvantage under which he laboured in both battles from want of cavalry. It was owing to this circumstance that the French, after the action of the 17th, were enabled to effect their retreat in good order, and the same cause saved their army from being completely routed and destroyed in that of the 21st. This is a serious charge against Ministers, and one which demands the most serious investigation. Should Junot still fight another battle

163

before he surrenders, every drop of British blood that shall be shed in it is chargeable upon the authors of this unaccountable and shameful neglect.'[5] The Opposition Press, while rejoicing in the victory, was determined not to allow any credit for it to go to the government. For the moment they were content to forget that Wellesley, the hero of the hour, was a minister.

The elation caused by the unaccustomed news of victory caused a wave of optimism to sweep the country. It was assumed that the war in the Peninsula was as good as over. On 7th September the *Chronicle* wrote, 'We hope and trust that our army in Portugal, reinforced by a body now embarking at Margate, Harwich and Cork, are intended to act in Italy. . . . We might safely count on the emancipation of Italy – a thing most truly to be desired.' The following day the paper continued on this theme, saying that 'Spain will in all probability effect her own deliverance without our aid, and Portugal, with our assistance, is likely soon to be rescued from the thraldom of her oppressors.'

For ten days after the publication of the Vimeiro dispatch no news of any kind arrived in England from the army in Portugal. Public enthusiasm and expectation had been raised to fever pitch and there was nothing on which it could be fed. The newspapers, therefore, resorted to publishing rumours which even they could not pretend to have any serious foundation. On 13th September it was reported that 'a rumour of an extraordinary nature was current yesterday. . . . It was said that Junot had played off a complete trick on our commanders, Upon his defeat by Sir Arthur Wellesley, or perhaps rather in anticipation of that event, he had entered into a convention with the Portuguese government, composed we suppose of those persons to whom the Prince Regent [of Portugal] had consigned the direction of the government upon his departure for the Brazils – to the terms of which our generals have refused to accede.' The following day this was surpassed by the story that 'it was rumoured yesterday, but obviously without authority, that Junot had contrived to escape in a small vessel from Portugal. The

164

thing is not so very improbable. Bonaparte, whom Junot endeavours to imitate in every particular, abandoned a French army in Egypt, when he saw no chance of its success; and Junot may feel himself warranted in following the example.'[6]

Dalrymple's first dispatch, dated 3rd September, reached Downing Street on 15th September. That morning reports reaching the newspapers had made it clear that something was wrong in Portugal. A letter written by an Oporto merchant on 3rd September and reported in the *Chronicle* stated flatly that 'our army has been inactive since the 21st ult.' The leader writers seized their opportunity. 'So long as we continued without arrivals from Portugal, the public mind was tranquil. No suspicion arose that anything had occurred to disappoint the nation of the proper fruits of the victories that Sir Arthur Wellesley had so arduously gained. The delay was attributed solely to the obstacle of adverse winds; but yesterday when news from Oporto to the 3rd instant had actually been received, and it was announced that up to that date no further progress had been made by our armies, a very serious gloom hung over the Metropolis. Conjectures were formed of the most harassing kind and they were rendered more painful by the silence of Ministers.'

Ministers had much to be silent about, for they had known of the terms of the Armistice since 3rd September. On that day the Portuguese minister in London had called at the Foreign Office to protest about these terms. He had learned of them from a letter from the Bishop of Oporto dated 28th August which included a copy of the agreement. The Bishop had protested, in the name of 'this Supreme Government, representing His Royal Highness', that neither they nor their general had been consulted in the negotiations, that the cease-fire line had necessitated Portuguese troops retiring from positions they already held, and that the French were to be permitted to 'take with them whatever Portuguese property they may think proper, . . . and that all persons attached to the French are at perfect liberty to depart with them and that it was permitted for the French troops to evacuate Portugal by way of Spain.'[7]

165

The British government were taken aback. Castlereagh wrote to his brother his belief that the copy of the Armistice 'is base forgery somewhere, and nothing can induce me to believe it genuine.'[8] The Prime Minister who, since it was the weekend, was in the country wrote pathetically to Castlereagh: 'I do not know how to express my astonishment and perplexity at the contents of the paper which purports to be the Convention made by Sir A. Wellesley and Kellermann. They may be the terms proposed by the latter: and yet the expectation that they could be entertained even for a moment seems to be so preposterous, that I could scarcely credit that a Frenchman would have possessed sufficient assurance to have proposed them. But it is impossible that any English officer could have sanctioned them. To suppose Sir A. Wellesley capable of making such a sacrifice of the interest, honour and good faith of his country and of his own good sense, would be an act of injustice that I should not forgive myself for being guilty towards him. I am sure I need not desire you, my dear Lord, to take the first moment you are able to relieve me from this cruel distress, and to solve this incomprehensible enigma.'[9]

Ministers proceeded to deny the whole affair. The Portuguese minister was blandly informed that 'the King could not permit himself to attach any credit to such a convention having been agreed to, under the relative circumstances in which his fleet and armies were placed, towards those of his enemies, at the time when it professes to bear date.'[10] Should the Portuguese allegations be true, as for the most part they were, Ministers were in an unenviable position. On the previous day Castlereagh had written to Dalrymple giving him new orders for the employment of the army but adding 'that it is not His Majesty's pleasure that you should consider the present instruction as depriving you of the latitude of discretion, which you now possess, in acting in such cases as the good of His Majesty's service may appear to you to demand, without waiting for express orders from home.'[11] Everything had been entrusted to Sir Hew's discretion and, if the Portuguese were to be believed, Sir Hew was not to be trusted.

166

Why no news of the Armistice reached England from the army before 15th September is a question to which no satisfactory answer can be given. The arrival within a week of letters from Oporto disposes of the 'adverse winds' explanation put about by the government at the time. Sir Hew was culpably negligent in not reporting to London before 3rd September but this cannot be the whole explanation. Other officers in the army undoubtedly wrote home. Wellesley wrote to Castlereagh about the Armistice on 23rd* and 30th August and to the Lord-Lieutenant of Ireland on 27th. Nothing reached England before Sir Hew's dispatch. Even if Sir Hew delayed all the army's mail until his dispatch was complete, and there is no suggestion that he did, it could be supposed that Admiral Cotton, who was also vitally concerned with the terms of the agreement, would not have forborne to write and dispatch a letter on the subject.

Ministers attempted to put a good face on the receipt of this disappointing, and for them disastrous, news. To celebrate the liberation of Portugal the saluting batteries were fired as if for a victory. Initial reaction in the Press was moderate in tone and, for the moment, Wellesley's new-won reputation was sufficient to protect him from attack. 'We are at last enabled to put an end to the anxiety of the public relative to the state of the war in Portugal, though not to gratify its utmost expectations. Yesterday at four o'clock, Captain Dalrymple [Dalrymple's aide-de-camp] arrived with intelligence that General Junot had agreed to evacuate Portugal. Nothing can be more unsatisfactory. After the decisive victory obtained by a British force of 17,000 men, of which only 10,000 or 11,000 were engaged and after the arrival of reinforcements, carrying the total of our army to 30,000 effective men, it was universally expected that the next account would be of an *unconditional surrender* on the part of the French. Instead of this, we are informed by Lord Castlereagh that Junot had agreed to *evacuate* Portugal. The public, instead of receiving the intelligence with those marks of joy which the news of victory

* This letter was certainly delayed somewhat before dispatch since Sir Arthur added a postscript to it dated 27th August.

never fails to inspire, shewed evident symptoms of disappointment and even of dejection. The Park and Tower guns were
fired; but many people, thinking the news from Portugal was
not sufficient to warrant this mark of exultation, ascribed it to
intelligence having been received of a naval victory over the
Russian fleet in the Baltic. These accounts seem to justify the
reports, which have for some days been circulating, respecting a
misunderstanding which is represented to have taken place between our military commanders in Portugal. Sir Arthur Wellesley, in particular, is mentioned as being extremely dissatisfied
with the proceedings since he was superceded, and it has been
said even that he was about to return home in disgust. But
whatever foundation there may be for the former part of the
rumour, the high character of this distinguished and gallant
officer makes it impossible to believe the latter. We understand
that when the capitulation was signed he was above twenty miles
distant from headquarters.'[12]

The actual terms of the armistice and convention were in the
papers on Saturday 17th September and, at once, opinion began
to turn against Wellesley in the shock of seeing what had been
agreed over his signature. The armistice and convention, wrote
the *Chronicle*, 'deeply and painfully interested the public
mind. . . . Could we have supposed the French general to have
sitten down for the purpose of inventing terms of an agreement
which should not only wipe off every stain which his character
had received from a previous defeat, but of transferring that
stain from his own to the British character, he could not have
done it more effectively than by the present convention. We
must say, however, that we are very much surprised to find the
name of Sir Arthur Wellesley affixed to a treaty of armistice,
the fifth article of which is, in fact, the basis upon which the
Definitive Convention was afterwards concluded.'

After the weekend Sir Arthur had been definitely cast as the
villain of the piece, the more so since Tory partisans had started
an unwise campaign to exculpate him. 'Not the least surprising
circumstance connected with the transaction is Sir Arthur Wellesley's signature being affixed to the armistice which is, if possible,

more scandalously disgraceful than the convention itself, for in it we find the neutrality of the port of Lisbon recognised for the Russian fleet, a stipulation which, thanks to the firmness of Sir Charles Cotton, was not finally sanctioned. The friends of Sir A. Wellesley, with a very natural anxiety for his reputation, are exceedingly desirous that, though he signed the armistice, it was with the utmost reluctance, and only in consequence of the express and peremptory orders of his commander. This explanation was circulated both on Saturday and yesterday with the utmost industry and zeal. One might hear it in every coffee room, and an evening paper on Sunday had a placard, in large letters, stuck up on the window of the office *"Sir Arthur Wellesley no party to the shameful convention"*. Do Sir Arthur's friends mean to give out that he was reduced to the level of one of Maillardet's machines, that he was nothing more than the *pen* in Sir Hew Dalrymple's hand, and that he had not even the power to annex to his signature, "by order of the commander." '[13]

The attack grew steadily in violence and was more and more directed at Wellesley. On 21st September, when the tirade had to compete for the headlines with the burning down of Covent Garden Theatre, the *Chronicle* demanded: 'Who, in the absence of all evidence, either positive or circumstantial, direct or collateral, will believe that Sir Arthur, a Minister of State, highly and powerfully connected, of a family certainly not distinguished for the meek submissiveness of their tempers, having just resigned the chief command of an army, which we are told had in the course of four days gained two decisive victories, would, in compliance to the mandate of Sir Hew Dalrymple, a person whom the world scarcely ever heard of, involuntarily subscribe an instrument at once of his own and his country's dishonour? Had he not approved it, we are convinced that he would, rather than sign it, have cut off his right hand, aye, that he would have submitted to have been shot in front of the camp, sooner than stoop to such ignominy.' Fuel was added to the fire by the Portuguese who were intent upon their revenge for the ignominious part they had played in both the fighting and the

169

negotiations. 'It is said that the Bishop of Oporto applied to Sir Arthur on his landing for 15,000 stand of arms, which were sent by government for the use of the Portuguese, and that he, rather in an ungracious manner, refused to deliver them – a circumstance which accounts for there being so few Portuguese in the two engagements. It is reported also that he refused to supply the Portuguese who accompanied the British army, although the latter was plentifully supplied.'*[14]

Before the end of the month the *Chronicle* was declaring, 'if the Wellesleys must be employed, for God's sake, let it henceforth be in regulating the police of the City of Dublin, or enforcing the residence of the Irish clergy.' On 4th October the Common Council of the City of London passed, *nemine contradicente*, a resolution 'that a humble and dutiful address and petition be presented to his Majesty expressing our grief and astonishment at the extraordinary convention lately entered into by the commanders of his Majesty's forces in Portugal and the Commander of the French forces in Lisbon; praying upon his Majesty to institute such an Inquiry into this dishonourable and unprecedented transaction, as will lead to the discovery and punishment of those by whose misconduct and incapacity the cause of the country and its allies has been so shamefully sacrificed.' Mr. Alderman Birch, from the depth of his military experience on Finsbury fields, said that he would be ashamed of himself, holding as he did his Majesty's commission in a Volunteer corps, if he did not give his assent to every word of the motion.

On the same day H.M.S. *Plover*, with Wellesley on board, anchored in Plymouth Sound. It was not a happy homecoming. An officer who had sailed in the *Plover* wrote that 'the inhabitants of Devonshire were so incensed by the Convention of Cintra that they seemed to have forgotten Roliça and Vimeiro, and consequently received Sir Arthur with every mark of dis-

* There was some sub-stratum of truth in the second accusation. Trant's 2,000 Portuguese did not receive British rations before Vimeiro but were fed from two small French ration stores captured by the British and handed over to the Portuguese.

170

approbation; indeed hissings and booings greeted him at every town and village of that county, through which he had to pass on the way to the metropolis.'[15]

Reaching London on 6th October, he saw for the first time Dalrymple's dispatch of 3rd September and the final form of the convention. Without delay, he wrote formally to Castlereagh complaining that in Dalrymple's dispatch 'it would appear, from an inaccuracy of expression, that I had agreed upon and signed certain articles "for the suspension of hostilities on the 22nd of August"; I beg leave to inform your lordship that I did not negotiate that agreement; that it was negotiated by his Excellency [Dalrymple] in person, with General Kellermann, in the presence of Lieut.-General Sir Harry Burrard and myself, and that I signed it by his Excellency's desire. But I could not consider myself responsible in any degree for the terms in which it was framed, or for any of its provisions.'[16] He added, however, that though he might disagree over the details, 'I concurred with the Commander of the Forces in thinking it expedient that the French army in Portugal should be allowed to evacuate that kingdom.'[17]

Two days later he had an interview with Castlereagh, intending to speak, as he had promised to do, in the interests of Moore. He found that it was unnecessary. He learned that Dalrymple had already been peremptorily recalled, Burrard was to follow and that the command had, in a letter of 25th September, been given to Moore. He wrote immediately to Moore offering to serve under him, 'than which nothing can be more satisfactory to me. I will go to Coruña immediately, where I hope to find you.' Before this letter was even sealed, he had to add a postscript. 'Since writing the above I find it will be necessary that I should wait in England till Sir Hew Dalrymple will return, and it will be known at what time the inquiry will be made into the late transactions in Portugal, on which I am to be examined. I will join you, however, at the moment I am set at liberty, for which I long most anxiously.'[18]

The attack on him by the newspapers did not worry him unduly. 'You will readily believe', he wrote to the Duke of

Richmond, 'that I was much surprised when I arrived in England to hear the torrents of abuse with which I have been assailed; and that I have been accused of every crime of which a man can be guilty, excepting cowardice. I have not read a word that has been written on either side, and don't mean to authorise the publication of a single line in my defence.'[19] He added that 'I think that Sir H. Dalrymple's letter of the 3rd September has, by fixing on me, by a purposed inaccuracy of expression, the odium of negotiating that instrument, enabled me to explain the share I had in it to the King's ministers and to the King,' but apart from the letter he had already written to Castlereagh when he first saw Dalrymple's letter he proposed to do nothing. 'The rest I shall leave to chance, and to the result of the inquiry into Sir H. Dalrymple's conduct.'

On 12th October the King held a levée at St. James's Palace and, in conversation with Castlereagh, Wellesley announced his intention of attending and asked the Secretary of State to take him there in his carriage. 'Castlereagh hemmed and hawed, and said there was so much ill-humour in the public mind that it might produce inconvenience, and, in short, he advised me not to go to the levée. I said: "When I first mentioned it, I only thought it a matter of respect and duty to the King; I now look upon it as a matter of self-respect and duty to my own character, and I therefore insist on knowing whether this advice proceeds in any degree from His Majesty, and I wish you distinctly to understand that I will go to the levée tomorrow, or I will never go to a levée in my life." Castlereagh immediately withdrew all opposition. I went, and was exceedingly well received by His Majesty.'[20]

In consequence of his insistence, Wellesley was present when the Lord Mayor and a deputation of the Common Council presented their petition against the 'extraordinary convention'. They met with a cold reception from the King. 'I am fully sensible', he said, 'of your loyalty and attachment to my person and government. I give credit to the motives which have dictated your Petition and Address; but I must remind you, that it is inconsistent with the principles of British justice to pronounce

172

judgment without previous investigation. I should have hoped that recent occurrences would have convinced you that I am at all times ready to institute inquiries on occasions in which the character of the country or the honour of my arms is concerned; and that the interposition of the City of London could not be necessary for inducing me to direct inquiries to be made into a transaction which has disappointed the hopes and expectations of the nation.'[21] After this dignified rebuke, the deputation, seeing Wellesley standing near, 'came up with fawning civility and expressed anxious wishes for his good health.'[22]

The King's kindly reception of Wellesley in contrast to his rebuff of the City was seized upon as evidence that Sir Arthur was to be protected by influence from the consequence of his ill-doing. *The Times* wrote: 'Is not a gracious reception at court no prejudication of a man against whom there are apparent, we do not say conclusive, proofs of guilt? Either a presentation at court is an honour, or it is not an honour: if it is not an honour, why are men presented at all? and if it is, why is a man presented, respecting whose conduct His Majesty assured the City of London, that a due inquiry is still to be made? Sir Arthur, therefore, is, it appears, to be acquitted, or rather has been acquitted. We are sorry for it; for those who perceive that he is prevailing by dint of influence, might have wished that he had, merely for experiment's sake, condescended to prevail by dint of innocence.'[23]

Nor did the rejection of the City's petition discourage other groups from following their examples. All over the country meetings were held to pass resolutions for addresses to be presented to the King. Such a meeting in Southampton was addressed by William Cobbett, who devoted his speech almost entirely to a personal attack on Wellesley and his family, quite overlooking the military merits or demerits of the case under consideration. 'It is evident to the whole nation that His Majesty's ministers are fully determined to screen Sir Arthur Wellesley. Sir Arthur Wellesley, it is well known, is allied to a family, the most powerful and eminent of any in this country – a family raised to predominance, not by any great or shining talents, nor by actions

173

of a sort that can be deemed even meritorious. They have beaten the poor Indians, just as dogs would do a flock of sheep out of a field. . . . Sir Arthur, before he left this country, enjoyed a salary of £6,566 for being Chief Secretary in Ireland. Ministers take him from that office and send him to Portugal as general. He still enjoys the emoluments of that office, although it was impossible for him to execute the duties of it. By all the powerful influence which that family enjoys in the House of Commons, for it is a fact that they have no less than twelve votes, Ministers find it in their interests to screen him. The other commanders, Ministers will perhaps endeavour to screen, for the sake of screening him. They know that if they bring the others to trial, they will probably impeach him. . . . I wish you to bear in mind that the Wellesley family actually at this moment receives out of this country the sum of £23,766 annually.* This sum you have to pay out of your pockets and it is a sum equal to the poor rate of sixty parishes on an average in England and Wales.'[24]

Wellesley refused to let the popular clamour alarm him. Back at the Chief Secretary's desk in Dublin Castle he wrote to General Spencer, still in Portugal, 'notwithstanding the calumny and abuse of which I am the object, for measures not my own, and against which I gave my opinion, I have neither lost my temper nor my spirits; and I look with pride and satisfaction at the confidence and kindness of yourself and the officers of the army who, after all, are the best judges of my conduct, and at the affection of my friends. The King, the Prince of Wales, and the Duke of York, received me most graciously; and I think I may defy the mob of London. The transactions in Portugal must be inquired into; and my intention is to wait with patience for the result of the inquiry, for my justification with the public. I shall adopt no illegitimate means of setting them right, and

---

* This figure is unlikely to be anywhere near the truth. At the time Wellesley's eldest brother, Lord Wellesley, held no office. William and Henry Wellesley were respectively Secretaries to the Navy and the Treasury, the salaries of which posts did not exceed £1,000 p.a. each. The remaining brother, Gerald, was a parson.

shall neither publish anything myself, nor authorise a publication by any one else.'[25] In particular he was anxious not to get Sir Harry Burrard 'into a scrape, not only out of regard for him, but because I think it fatal to the public service to expose officers to the treatment which I have received, and to punishment for acting upon their own military opinions, which they may fairly entertain.'[26]

His feelings about Sir Hew Dalrymple were less charitable. He had heard from Sir William Scott that 'Sir Hew makes no scruple of saying that, be the Convention bad or be it good, it is no measure of his; that it is all Sir Arthur Wellesley's; that the whole measure was Sir Arthur's; that the Armistice was negotiated between Sir Arthur and Kellermann; that he scarcely put in a word or made any objection to anything; that in this he acted according to his instructions, which were to consult Sir Arthur in everything, and to be guided by his opinions.'[27] It was obvious that Sir Hew intended to make the most of the clamour in the Press against Wellesley.

On 1st November the government finally made public its determination to set up a Board of Inquiry to look into the transactions in Portugal, to give its opinions of them and to state 'their opinion whether any or what further proceedings should be had thereupon.'

*　　*　　*

Napoleon is said to have observed, on hearing the news of the establishment of the Board of Inquiry, that he was grateful to the British for putting their generals on trial since it saved him from having to bring his old friend Junot to a court-martial. To judge from his correspondence, his reaction to the whole business of Portugal was to treat it with one of the displays of indifference which he reserved for disasters about which he could do nothing. Although Junot had been inept in his handling of Vimeiro, the loss of Portugal was the natural result of the Emperor's neglect. He had sent Junot to Lisbon with too small a corps. He had forbidden Junot to do anything which might reconcile Portugal to French rule. Although he had recognised, in October 1807, that the British, with their long standing alliance with, and large commercial interests in Portugal, might intervene he took no subsequent steps to guard against the landing of a British army. Apart from 4,000 drafts who did little more than make good the wastage in Junot's ranks, he sent no reinforcements.

He gave orders from Milan before Christmas 1807 that Dupont's corps of 25,000 men should be added to the Army of Portugal, its pay and rations being a charge to Portuguese funds.[28]. That corps, however, was retained in Spain for no immediate military purpose until it was used for the French entry into Madrid in March 1808 and from where it set off on its disastrous march to Bailen. So little did Napoleon reckon that Junot needed reinforcement that as late as the end of May he was ordered to detach 4,000 men to Cadiz to help Dupont and given the comforting assurance that 'you have nothing serious to fear from the English.'[29] This was the last letter which Junot received from Paris. Much of it was taken up with plans for a French naval expedition to Brazil, of which country the Emperor required maps, plans and information.

When the news of the loss of Portugal reached him in detail he treated Junot with uncharacteristic generosity, writing to him, 'You have done nothing dishonourable; you have brought back my troops, my eagles and my artillery. I had, however, hoped that you would do better. . . . You won the convention by your courage, not by your dispositions, and the English are right to complain that their general signed it. . . . There is, however, one point in the Convention which is difficult to justify – you abandoned Elvas; why did you not reinforce the garrison and order them to hold out until their last crumb of bread? We shall be back at Elvas before the end of December; it would have been a great help to have found the fortress held for us.'[30]

It was the summer of 1811 before French troops saw Elvas again. It was only a distant, fleeting view. On the other hand, sixteen of the battalions which had fought under Junot

176

in Portugal formed part of Soult's corps when, on 16th January 1809, he attacked Sir John Moore at Coruña.

References

Chapter 9.   'This dishonourable and unprecedented transaction'

1   Malmesbury ii 78
2   MC 3 Sept '08
3   MC 5 Sept '08
4   WD iv 108. HB to Castlereagh, 21 Aug '08
5   MC 5 Sept '08
6   MC 14 Sept '08
7   HD 310. Bishop of Oporto to Portuguese Minister, 28 Aug '08
8   CC vi 423. Castlereagh to Charles Stewart, 4 Sept '08
9   CC vi 423. Portland to Castlereagh, 4 Sept '08, noon
10   HD 121
11   HD 109. Castlereagh to HD, 2 Sept '08
12   MC 16 Sept '08
13   MC 19 Sept '08
14   MC 27 Sept '08
15   Ross Lewin i 246
16   WD iv 161. AW to Castlereagh, 6 Oct '08
17   ib
18   SD vi 151. AW to Moore, 10 Oct '08
19   SD vi 151. AW to Richmond, 10 Oct '08
20   Croker i 344
21   MC 13 Oct '08
22   Stanhope 243
23   *The Times*, 14 Oct '08
24   MC 4 Nov '08
25   SD vi 168. AW to Spencer, 22 Oct '08
26   SD vi 153. AW to Buckingham, 11 Oct '08
27   SD vi 164. Pole to AW, 19 Oct '08
28   NC xvi 13409. Decree of 23 Dec '07
29   NC xvii 14023. N to Junot, 29 May '08
30   NC xviii 14386. N to Junot, 19 Oct '08

'Considering the Extraordinary

O^N Monday 14th November 'the Board of General Officers appointed to inquire into the Convention &c in Portugal' met in the Great Hall of Chelsea College (Chelsea Hospital). General Sir David Dundas was in the chair and with him sat six other officers, three generals and three lieutenant-generals. Dundas was the most respected officer in the army. He had served widely over the western hemisphere since he joined the army in 1756 and was the author of the standard drill book of the army. He was Colonel of the 2nd Dragoons and Governor of Chelsea Hospital. His senior colleague, General the Earl of Moira, had distinguished himself in a moderate way in the American war but had seen little active service since the Flanders campaign at the beginning of the French Revolutionary war. He was Constable of the Tower and Colonel of the Twenty-Seventh Foot. The remainder of the Board, General Peter Craig, General Lord Heathfield, Lieutenant-Generals Lord Pembroke, Sir George Nugent Bt., and Oliver Nicholls were all respectable soldiers in a modest way with records of reliable service in the American war and little active service since. They were the best that could be got together at short notice, bearing in mind that they must be demonstrably free from political bias. Dundas, the oldest

Circumstances'

member of the board, was seventy, and the youngest was Lord
Pembroke at forty-nine. All of them were senior to Burrard and
Wellesley but the three lieutenant-generals were junior to Dal-
rymple. None of them had any experience of holding the post of
Commander-in-Chief of an expeditionary force of the size of
Wellesley's army at Vimeiro; indeed, of all living British officers
only Field-Marshal the Duke of York had such experience.

Since Castlereagh had laid it down that 'until the court meets,
no person can be summoned regularly as a witness',[1] the first
session was unproductive. 'His Majesty's Warrant . . . having
been read in public court, and no papers or information being
then before the Board, the court was ordered to be cleared.'[2]
Having made requests for all relevant papers to be produced,
all the requisite witnesses summoned and for the 'several
lieutenant-generals who commanded at different periods in
Portugal' to submit narratives of their proceedings, the Board
adjourned until the following Thursday.

When the Board resumed it had a great mass of documents;
over two hundred orders, dispatches and letters were to be laid
before it. On that day also there appeared before it Sir Hew
Dalrymple and Sir Arthur Wellesley. Sir Harry Burrard had not

yet reached England from Portugal. It was not until almost four weeks later that Sir Harry made his first appearance on 13th December. Sir Harry, in any case, was not important in the proceedings. He had returned to being the gallant, amiable nonentity that, but for an unfortunate quirk of the seniority list, he should have remained for the rest of his life. In his twenty-four hours of command only one point of subsequent importance emerged. Should he have sanctioned Wellesley's proposal to advance when the French retreated beaten from Vimeiro? He gave many reasons for declining to do so, of which the most remarkable was having observed a formed body of French infantry standing near the Torres Vedras road ready to cover the French retreat. No such body existed, although there is no doubt that Sir Harry, who was not a man to lie, believed, in December, that he had seen them. A number of witnesses were examined by Sir Arthur about this nebulous French reserve, none of them had seen it except General Spencer, who claimed to have seen 'one line distinctly formed, about three miles, . . . in front of the centre of our position, where they remained, I think, upwards of one hour.'[3] After the court had adjourned for the day, Wellesley asked him about this piece of his evidence. ' "Why, Spencer, I never heard of this reserve before. How is it that you only mention it now?" "Oh", said he, "poor Burrard has so large a family." I had no desire to give pain or trouble either to Burrard or Spencer, who was a very odd sort of man, and I did not urge any questions on this point before the Court.'[4]

The nominal business of the Board was to decide who was responsible for the Armistice and the Convention and to recommend to the government whether anyone had behaved criminally or dishonourably in doing so. In reality the proceedings of the Board developed into a duel between Dalrymple and Wellesley, with the Board acting as umpire, occasionally putting in a few questions to one or the other contestants.

In theory nothing could be clearer than Dalrymple's responsibility. There might be extenuating circumstances, not least Burrard's rejection of Wellesley's plan to reach Lisbon before the French by advancing as soon as Junot's attack had been

180

broken twenty-four hours before Dalrymple landed in Portugal. Nevertheless, at the time of the signature of both documents, he was Commander-in-Chief. The Convention bore his signature in ratification. The Armistice had been negotiated and signed in his presence. Despite this, he had great and real advantages. In the first place the members of the Board were likely, almost instinctively, to be in sympathy with him. They were all worthy, honourable men of modest ability who in the traditional way of professional soldiers in any army at any time, tended to close the ranks and show a solid front in the face of a civilian uproar. Sir Hew was very much one of themselves. Any one of the Board might well have found themselves in his position and they must have wondered whether, in the circumstances, they would have performed better. Each of them could imagine the dismay with which they would have received Castlereagh's well-meaning but unfortunate letter commending Wellesley 'as an officer of whom it is desirable, on all accounts, to make the most prominent use.' (see p. 67) None of them would doubt that Sir Hew would have been only too happy to leave the difficult decisions to Sir Arthur, secure in the knowledge that by doing so he was only obeying his orders. Being senior generals, they would also have realised, as civilians and politicians did not, how difficult the decisions would have been to a newly arrived commander, short of information and at the head of an army which was resentful of his arrival and pointedly loyal to its former, victorious general. It was unlikely that a Board so constituted would wish to make any soldier a scapegoat. If it was forced to do so, if public opinion insisted that someone should be thrown to the lions, they would have preferred to blame Wellesley, who was something of an outsider in military circles in England and whose downfall could be cushioned by his family and political connections. Sir Hew had neither wealth nor influence.

Dalrymple's second advantage was the malignancy of public opinion against Wellesley. The Parliamentary opposition had been sedulous in circulating anti-Wellesley stories in an endeavour to discredit the government in general and in particular the influential Wellesley faction. It was not only the Press who violently attacked Wellesley, the intellectuals reached for their pens. Wordsworth wrote a tract, a sonnet, and addressed a public meeting on the subject. Lord Byron dashed off two more cantos for *Childe Harold*, raising a most unfortunate precedent.

'Where was the pity of our sires for Byng?'

Although Sir Walter Scott wished earnestly that Wellesley was still at the head of the army in the Peninsula, the public was almost unanimous in casting Sir Arthur as the culprit. If Sir Hew could stomach being described as 'a person whom the world scarcely ever heard of', he stood a fair chance of being exonerated.

This chance he decided to take. He decided to shelter behind Wellesley's political influence whatever the cost to his own self esteem. Whatever had been done, he claimed, had been done by Wellesley's advice and with his consent. In this he was greatly aided by the character of his opponent. Utterly incapable of telling a lie, Wellesley had agreed, on the day on which the Armistice was signed, to the paramount importance of securing the evacuation of the French from Portugal without further military operations on a large scale. He could be trusted to say as much before the Board and, granted this admission, Sir Hew could, by innuendo and embroidery, confirm the Board in the belief, to which they were already half inclined, that Sir Hew had merely followed the advice which the Secretary of State had urged him to take. There is no reason to believe that, until his recall from Portugal, Sir Hew was not an honest and worthy man, serving his country to the best of his limited abilities. The storm that greeted him on his return to England had come as a complete surprise. He believed then, and continued to believe until his death, that he had acted properly and for the best. In November, however, he was a badly frightened man. It was less than a year since Whitelocke had been court-martialled and disgraced for his failure at Buenos Aires (*see p.* 15). It was not quite fifty-two years since Admiral Byng had been shot on his own quarterdeck for what amounted to no more than an error of judgment. Sir Hew's probity was not of the same unyielding quality as Sir Arthur's. Faced with the prospect of disgrace or worse, he was willing to bend the truth as far as he safely could, taking care only to make no statement that Wellesley could prove to be untrue. It would not be a creditable performance but, with care, it should be credible.

Wellesley's position, in theory, was as secure as Dalrymple's was vulnerable. All that could be held against him was that, in the Commander-in-Chief's presence and at his request, he had put his name to the Armistice. Nothing about the final Convention could be attributed to him except insofar as it was a logical sequel to the Armistice. All that could be charged against him was that he had given bad advice. This could not, by any stretch of the imagination, be built up into a court-martial offence. In practice, however, the positions were largely reversed. Few people cared very strongly what happened to Dalrymple. There were many who would have been delighted to see the downfall of a Wellesley. Samuel Whitbread, M.P., wrote that he was, 'not sorry to see the Wellesley pride lowered a little',[5] and William Cobbett wrote to Lord Folkestone: 'How the devil will they get over this? Now we have the rascals on the hip. It is evident that *he* [Sir Arthur] was the prime cause – the *only* cause – of all the mischief, and that from the motive of thwarting everything *after he was superseded*. Thus do we pay for the arrogance of that damned infernal family.'[6]

Sir Arthur's disadvantages were, mainly, the converse of Dalrymple's advantages. Despite his two victories, it was around his head that the storm of public anger was playing. He would be the most acceptable scapegoat. Similarly, he would have less, if any, sympathy from the members of the Board. Generals have always mistrusted their political masters and, at a time when there were at least two hundred more generals than there could ever be commands available,* it could scarcely be wondered at if senior officers resented the cabinet's appointment of one of their own members, a man with little experience of European warfare and too young to have shared the bitterness of defeat in

* In the Army List for 1st November 1808 there are listed 2 Field-Marshals, 70 Generals, 130 Lieutenant-Generals and 167 Major-Generals.

America, to a command which most of them would dearly have loved for themselves. Since the public outcry was largely a matter for politicians, the political general might be thought to be the best whipping boy.

Moreover, Sir Arthur's personality did not make his situation easy for him. His shyness tended to drive him to something approaching icy contempt when his own motives and actions were impugned. On the other hand, among friends and in moments of temper, he was liable to be too outspoken. In his private correspondence he alluded to 'Dowager Dalrymple and Betty Burrard' and these nicknames may well have come to the ears of the Board. Nor, since it was the common talk of the army in Portugal, can the Board have failed to hear of his very audible aside to his staff after Burrard had refused to sanction an advance after Vimeiro. Two versions were current. One has already been given (*see p.* 123): 'You may think about dinner, for there is nothing more for soldiers to do this day.' The other may also be true. 'Now we can go and shoot red-legged partridges.' A reputation for that kind of insubordination would weigh heavily against him at the Inquiry.

These were not his only grounds for concern. His political position could easily become a source of weakness. The government was not a strong one. If the outcry became a source of serious danger to the cabinet's survival they might easily jettison him as a political liability. Castlereagh was his friend, despite his hesitations over the levée, but Castlereagh was at growing enmity with Canning, a more influential figure, and Canning would not hesitate to sacrifice a colleague, or even a friend, to secure his own political future. Wellesley, who had realised from the start the possible consequences of signing the Armistice, must have realised that even if the Court of Inquiry cleared him, his career could be brought to an abrupt halt if, after a decent pause, he was quietly dropped from office. It is clear from his letter to Castlereagh dated 5th September (*see p.* 152) that he thought it possible that he would have been dropped as soon as the news of the Armistice reached England.

One consolation Sir Arthur did have. Four of the generals

who served under him at Vimeiro, together with his personal staff were available to give evidence on his behalf. In addition Captain Pulteney Malcolm, who as captain of H.M.S. *Donegal* had been the senior naval officer directly co-operating with the army, had sought and obtained the Admiralty's permission to remain in England to give evidence. Sir Arthur could safely count on these witnesses staunchly supporting him, although none of them had been present at the negotiations for the armistice. Neither Dalrymple nor Burrard could call such telling witnesses since the staffs who served them were now acting in the same capacity for Sir John Moore, whose army was, while the Board sat, concentrating at Salamanca.

Dalrymple went straight into the attack. In his opening statement he started by complaining of a newspaper article 'calculated to load my character with gross and accumulated obloquy, for the purpose of rescuing a more favoured officer from the unlooked for unpopularity of a matter he most certainly approved. . . . The calumny I anxiously wish to repel is the unjust imputation that I had on the very day I landed in Portugal, the stupid presumption to meditate the impracticable design of compelling (as this figurative writer expresses it) "the hand that so recently had torn the laurel from the boastful French army, to become the instrument to attest the altered fortunes of his country, and the disappointment and degradation of his own victorious hands." '[7] The implication that Wellesley had inspired such articles was clear.

Having prefaced his remarks with this damaging innuendo, Sir Hew proceeded to launch his main contention – that the Armistice was Wellesley's doing and that he had throughout been guided by his advice. 'I beg leave most solemnly to affirm upon the word and honour of an officer that the conference at Vimeiro with the French General Kellermann . . . was carried on by Sir Harry Burrard,* Sir Arthur Wellesley and myself; that all and each one of us seemed to offer whatever observations we thought

* A week later, on 24th November, some qualm of conscience moved Dalrymple to admit in evidence that 'Sir Harry Burrard did not seem to me to take an active part in the discussion.' (Cintra 121).

185

proper, but that Sir Arthur appeared to me to bear that prominent part in the discussion, which the situation he so lately filled, the victory he had so recently gained, and his own more perfect information upon many most important, though local and incidental circumstances, gave him a just right to assume.'[8]

Wellesley then replied to Dalrymple's opening address asking that he be permitted 'to make a few observations upon the paper which has been read by Sir Hew Dalrymple. I have as much reason to complain as he has, that the writers in the newspapers should for some weeks past have amused the public with supposed accounts and comments on the late transactions in Portugal, and most particularly that they should have ventured to state some of them from what they call authority from me or my friends. I never said nor never authorised any body to say, and more I can venture to say, that no person connected with me, as my relations, friends or aides-de-camp, or otherwise in the service, ever gave any authority to any publisher of a newspaper, or any body else to declare, that I was compelled to sign, or even ordered to sign the paper to which my name appears. It is true I was present when the Armistice was negotiated by the Commander-in-Chief, and I did assist in his negotiations, and I signed it by desire of the Commander-in-Chief; but I never said and never will say, that the expression of the desire of the Commander-in-Chief was in the shape of an order, which it was not in my power to disobey, much less of compulsion.

'I thought it my duty to comply with this desire of the Commander-in-Chief from the wish which I have always felt, according to which I have always acted, to carry into effect the orders and objects of those placed in command over me, however I might differ in opinion with them. I certainly did differ in opinion with the Commander-in-Chief upon more than one point in the detail of what I was thus called upon to sign, as I shall shew hereafter; but as I concurred in and advised the adoption of the principle of the measure, viz. that the French should be allowed to evacuate Portugal, . . . I did not think it

186

proper to refuse to sign the paper on account of my disagreement on the details.'[9]

It was a dignified and effective reply. It was indeed the only effective reply that he could make. It was the reply of an officer loyal to his superior however much he might disagree with him. It also showed that, whatever the political and public clamour against allowing the French to evacuate rather than insisting that they be prisoners of war, he was not afraid to reaffirm his opinion which, as he showed, was based on good military grounds.

The Board continued its meetings with occasional adjournments until 26th November, when it adjourned itself 'till Tuesday se'nnight, the 6th of December', since Burrard had still not arrived. Up to that point the pattern had been constant. Dalrymple consistently tried to put the whole odium on to Sir Arthur, who patiently accepted responsibility only for those parts which he had advised. Once, when the duration of the cease-fire was being discussed, he came near to losing his temper. 'First, I am called the negotiator of this instrument, and in this important point the plan of the French general is adopted instead of mine. But, secondly, I am called the adviser of these measures, and for this crime I am here. Now, although I must submit to incur disgrace and punishment, where I shall be found to deserve these misfortunes, I must say that I think it is a new measure of punishment invented for me; that I, a subordinate officer, am to be punished for advising measures which were not conducted according to my advice.'[10] For the rest, he maintained that icy calm which was to become so misleading a part of his public image.

Once he was able to pin a lie on to Sir Hew. When referring to the actual signing of the armistice, Sir Hew had said: 'It is quite true that when the treaty was being copied fair, I was approaching the table to sign it myself; General Kellermann observed that I could not, as General-in-Chief, sign preliminary articles with him, as General of Division.'[11] Wellesley replied, 'I am afraid that Sir Hew Dalrymple's memory has not served him well on this occasion; . . . if this question was asked after the instrument had been drawn up, and General Dalrymple was

187

about to sign it, he was about to sign it without reading the instrument; for, if he had read it, he would have seen my name was used in it.'[12] By 23rd November Wellesley was satisfied that he had made his case so strong that Sir Hew had been forced to 'relieve me from the responsibility of negotiating the Armistice.'[13]

On that day he wrote to a friend: 'The Court of Inquiry are going on as well as I could wish. I made my statement respecting the Armistice and Convention yesterday; and I was obliged to go further into the subject than I intended, owing to the attacks which Sir Hew Dalrymple had made upon me, not only in the opening of the Court, but in his narrative of the proceedings. The consequence is that he can't escape censure. If he had done what a gentleman ought to have done, . . . and if he had not attacked me when he first addressed the Court, and in his narrative, I should have defended him for the measure of allowing the French to evacuate Portugal, and should not have said one word about the details of the Convention. I can only hope that Burrard will be a little more fair, or a little more candid, than Sir Hew has been.'[14]

When Sir Harry finally appeared before the Board on 13th December, he was so fair and candid that the proceedings became something of an anti-climax. On the only question on which he was really concerned, he admitted making an error of judgment in refusing to allow Ferguson's brigade to advance to secure Solignac's battalions as prisoners. On the main point he could only say that he had acted according to his judgment. That this was true no one could doubt and Wellesley, in his final statement to the Board remarked, 'although I did differ, and still do differ, in opinion with Lieutenant-General Sir Harry Burrard, respecting the measures adopted immediately after the battle of 21st August, I hope it will not be deemed presumptuous in me as an inferior officer to declare to the Court and the Public the opinion which I have always entertained that Sir Harry Burrard decided upon that occasion upon fair military grounds, in the manner which appeared to him to be most conducive to the interests of the country; and that he had no motive which could be supposed

188

personal to me, or which as an officer he could not avow.'[15] The implication was, perhaps, that he would not care to have to avow the same purity for Dalrymple's conduct and motives.

The last evidence was heard on 14th December and eight days later the Board presented its report to the King. The report first rehearsed the history of the campaign and then gave what, for want of a better name, must be called its conclusions.

'ON THE WHOLE,

'It appears that the operations of the army under Sir Arthur Wellesley from his landing at Mondego Bay the 1st of August until the conclusion of the action at Vimeiro the 21st of August, were highly honourable and successful, and such as might have been expected from a distinguished general at the head of a British army of 13,000 men, augmented on the 20th and 21st to 17,000, deriving only some small aid from a Portuguese corps (1,600), and against whom an enemy not exceeding 14,000 men in the field was opposed. And this before the arrival of a very considerable reinforcement from England under Lieutenant-General Sir John Moore, which however did arrive, and join the army from the 25th to the 30th August.

'It appears a point on which no evidence adduced can enable the Board to pronounce with confidence, whether or not a pursuit after the battle of the 21st could have been efficacious, nor can the Board feel competent to determine on the expedience of a forward movement to Torres Vedras, when Sir Harry Burrard has stated weighty considerations against such a measure. Further it is to be observed that so many collateral circumstances could not be known in the moment of the enemy's repulse, as afterwards became clear to the army, and have been represented to the Board. And considering the extraordinary circumstances under which two Commanding Generals arrived from the ocean and joined the army (the one during, and the other immediately after a battle, and those successively superceding each other, and both the original Commander within the space of twenty-four hours),

189

it is not surprising that the army was not carried forward until the second day after the action, from the necessity of the Generals being acquainted with the actual state of things, and of their army, and proceeding accordingly.

'It appears that the Convention of Cintra, in its progress and conclusion, or at least the principal articles of it, were not objected to by the five distinguished Lieutenant-Generals of that army, and other General Officers who were on that service, whom we have had the opportunity to examine, have also concurred in the great advantages, that were immediately gained, to the country of Portugal, to the army and navy, and to the general service, by the conclusion of the Convention at that time.

'On a consideration of all circumstances, as set forth in this report, we most humbly submit our opinion, that no further military proceeding is necessary on the subject; because howsoever some of us may differ in our sentiments respecting the fitness of the Convention in the relative situation, it is our unanimous declaration that unquestionable zeal and firmness appear throughout by Lieutenant-Generals Sir Hew Dalrymple, Sir Harry Burrard, and Sir Arthur Wellesley, as well as the ardour and gallantry of the rest of the Officers and Soldiers on every occasion during this expedition have done honour to the troops, and reflected lustre on your Majesty's arms.'[16]

It is hard to see what other finding could have been reached by the Board. Their conclusions meant, in short, that Wellesley had done well and that Dalrymple and Burrard had done their best. The key phrase was that which referred to 'the extraordinary circumstances under which two Commanding Generals arrived from the ocean and joined the army (the one during, the other immediately after a battle, and those successively superseding each other, and both the original Commander within the space of twenty-four hours)'. This was an implied criticism of the government which created the 'extraordinary circumstances', but, as the Board must have realised even the government was a prisoner of the system within which it was bound to work. Everything about the British system of waging war was so cumbrous that it was a triumph, if any operation happened at the right place and at the right time. No one would claim to dispute the cabinet's right to choose the commander-in-chief of the expedition. Their original choice of Wellesley had been amply justified while the force was small. As soon, however, as the expeditionary force was reinforced to 30,000 men, the 'customs of the service' made it impossible to keep Wellesley in command. Owing to the remarkable system of promoting generals the choice of senior officers was extremely limited, if they were to be under sixty and acceptable to both politicians and soldiers. The cabinet, which itself contained two generals senior to Wellesley, chose Dalrymple on the perfectly reasonable grounds that he knew most of the situation in the Peninsula. It was an honest choice, if an unwise one.

Stretching their prerogative slightly the cabinet then insisted on the appointment of a second-in-command. They had no right to nominate a subordinate commander, nor did they attempt to do so, but they claimed the right to have an interim commander appointed so as to prevent the command of a large army falling into the hands of a man in whom they, collectively, had no confidence. That they were wrong in having no confidence in Sir John Moore is irrelevant. No government can be expected to permit their principal army to be in the hands of a man whom they distrust.

The absurdity of three commanders-in-chief in three days was not the government's fault or intention. It arose from a freak of the wind which brought Dalrymple from Gibraltar only twenty-four hours after it had brought Burrard from England. By all expectations, Sir Hew would have been likely to arrive about a fortnight after Sir Harry.

Reasonable or not, the Board's report did not please the authorities. It was returned to them with a request from the Duke of York that the members should state individually their opinions on the desirability and terms of both the Armistice and the Convention. Three members recorded their view that the Con-

191

vention was too liberal to the French. Of these, two, Oliver Nicholls and Lord Pembroke believed that the Armistice was justified on the grounds that during its duration a reinforcement of 10,000 men landed to support the British while no such resources were available to the French. Only Lord Moira deplored both Armistice and Convention. The Armistice he opposed, as Wellesley had done, in that it contained the written outline of the Convention. The Convention terms he thought too easy. 'Had it not been practicable to reduce the French army to lay down its arms unconditionally, still an obligation not to serve for a specified time might have been insisted upon, or Belleisle might have been prescribed as the place at which they should have been landed, in order to prevent the possibility of their reinforcing (at least for a long time) the armies employed for the subjugation of Spain.'[17]

There was clearly nothing further that could be done in the way of 'further military proceedings' in view of the Board's report but it was not to be expected that government or people would be content with allowing Dalrymple to go scot-free. George III was certainly not content. His Majesty, in a memorandum which he sent to the Secretary of State to be passed to Sir Hew through the commander-in-chief, expressed his disapprobation of those articles 'in which stipulations are made affecting the interests or feelings of the Spanish and Portuguese nations', and deemed it necessary 'that his sentiments should be clearly understood, as to the impropriety and danger of the unauthorised admission, into Military Conventions, of articles of such a description, which especially when incautiously framed, may lead to the most injurious consequences.

'His Majesty cannot forbear further to observe, that Lieutenant-General Sir Hew Dalrymple's delaying to transmit, for his information, the Armistice concluded on the 22nd August, until the 4th [sic] September; when he, at the same time, transmitted the ratified Convention, was calculated to produce great public inconvenience, and that such public inconvenience did, in fact, result therefrom.'[18]

To Dalrymple it seemed that this 'severe censure . . . addressed to me in the King's name, *and to me only*'[19] was unjust, that he was being made a scapegoat. In this Sir Hew was unreasonable. The Board of Inquiry had confined itself to military matters. The two points raised by the King were political. Tiresome and ineffective as they were, the Portuguese had been treated in the most cavalier fashion. Even if, as seems admissable, it was impracticable to consult Freire when the Armistice was being discussed, it was negligent and impolite not to consult him over the Definitive Convention. National policy and common-sense demanded that the officer responsible should be publicly reprimanded, even if only to repair the harm done to the Anglo-Portuguese alliance. Dalrymple was equally negligent in omitting to report to London for a fortnight after he had taken command. It may be that, for some reason, his report, like Wellesley's letters, would not have reached London before his eventual dispatch but this would not excuse him from having tried to keep the government informed.

It is hard to have much sympathy with Dalrymple. Admitting that an unfortunate chance threw him into a situation for which he was quite unfitted; allowing also that up to the time of his recall he had acted honestly according to his judgment, his attempt, when he realised that he had stirred up a political storm, to shuffle the responsibility on to his subordinate was discreditable in the extreme. Like Burrard he was unfit for his assignment, but, unlike Burrard, who behaved throughout most honourably, he malignantly tried to shift the blame. He was relieved of his Lieutenant-Governorship at Gibraltar and was never employed again.

As soon as the Board had concluded its proceedings, Wellesley returned to his office in Ireland. He began, not that he cared, to return to popular favour. The Mayor, Commonalty and Citizens of Londonderry and the Master, Wardens and Brethren of the Corporation of Cooks elected him as a Freeman. The City and County of Limerick presented him with addresses thanking him 'for his conduct whilst conducting His Majesty's forces in Portugal.' He replied to each, acknowledging the 'discipline and gallantry of the troops.'

The Opposition Press continued to snipe at him. The *Annual Register* wrote: 'In short, the report of the Board was an indirect censure on Sir Arthur; for if Sir Harry Burrard was justified under all the circumstances in not advancing until the arrival of reinforcements under Sir John Moore, Sir Arthur Wellesley, who knew he must be speedily reinforced, judged ill in pushing forward and exposing himself to an attack. . . . It was generally believed, and it was probably the truth, that Sir Arthur, confiding in the bravery of his troops, burned with a desire to have a brush with the French, before he should be superseded in command.'

The same line was followed when Castlereagh, in the House of Commons, moved a motion of thanks to Wellesley for the victory of Vimeiro. Several members, including Samuel Whitbread and the future Lord Melbourne, while not opposing the motion, commented that Burrard's name ought to be added. To this Castlereagh replied that 'all the military merit of this campaign was exclusively Wellesley's. No one was less disposed than himself to hurt the feelings of Sir Harry Burrard, than whom he did not believe there was a more gallant officer or one of a more enlarged soul, in the British Empire. But it would, in his opinion, be doing an injury to that gallant and meritorious officer, to mix him in the vote moved for.' Only Lord Folkestone, from the Opposition benches, actually opposed the motion. He did not think the victory 'to be of so brilliant description as to be entitled to a vote of thanks; as it fell short of any good consequences; and as the whole of the expedition ended in a manner disgraceful to the country. The Court of Inquiry could not blame Sir Harry Burrard for objecting to the advance of our forces. The immediate consequences of that objection were the Armistice and Convention; of the necessity of agreeing to which our generals would not have been reduced, if Sir Arthur had waited for only one day for the reinforcements under Sir John Moore, and not have been in such haste to bring on the battles of Roliça and Vimeiro.'[20] No one supported Lord Folkestone and his was the only dissentient voice when the vote was taken. In the House of Lords a similar motion was passed unanimously.

194

On the following day Lord Henry Petty moved to disapprove the Armistice and Convention. The finding of the Board carried no weight with him. 'With whatever respect he might regard the individual and military characters of the persons who composed the Board of Inquiry . . . constituted as that Board was, and its functions directed, it was a tribunal more incompetent to give satisfaction to the country, more irreconcilable with the known and received principles of law and equity, than any that ever existed.' Most of the blame, Lord Henry assigned to ministers. They had sent the expedition short of cavalry and of horses for the artillery, but their greatest fault was to send it to Portugal. 'There was nothing in the possession of the port of Lisbon that could be a source of immediate succour to the Spaniards; nothing connected with the real interests of even our faithful ally, the Queen of Portugal, or her subjects in Portugal.' Since, as he pointed out, ministers had left Wellesley's discretion to choose the place at which the landing should take place, the immediate fault was Sir Arthur's. Seconding the motion, General Banastre Tarleton, a veteran and eccentric relic of the American wars, directed his attack at Wellesley. The threat of being superseded had made him rash, 'he thought he could convince that honourable officer that there was something rash in the action of the 17th August, and something wrong in that of the 21st.'[21] The motion was defeated by 203 votes to 153.

These were just the mouthings of ignorant and factious politicians. The public had lost interest in Vimeiro and Cintra. Late on the evening of 22nd January, Lieutenant-General Lord Paget reached London from Coruña 'with an account of an attack made by the French, on Monday last, on a part of our army at Coruña, in which the French were driven back after a contest of three hours. Sir John Moore was killed during the action, and Sir David Baird lost an arm. . . . Our troops displayed their usual gallantry. Before Lord Paget left the fleet, all our army except 3,100 men were embarked.'[22] The British were indulging in their habit of gallant evacuation again.

On 10th March another French army, under Marshal Soult, started the second invasion of Portugal. On the 2nd April

195

Wellesley was informed that 'His Majesty . . . has thought fit
to select you [for] the command of His Majesty's forces in
Portugal.' He was to replace Sir John Craddock, whom Moore
had left as interim commander at Lisbon, and who had been
appointed to Dalrymple's old post at Gibraltar. Before sailing
he sought urgent instructions as to what course he should follow
should he find that Craddock had defeated the French. 'In the
event of General Craddock's success in any repulse of the enemy,
Sir Arthur could not reconcile it to his feelings to supersede
him.'[23]

*   *   *

On 1st July 1814 Arthur, Duke of Wellington, Marquis and
Earl of Wellington in Somerset, Viscount Wellington of Talavera,
Baron Douro of Wellesley, in the peerage of the United Kingdom, Duke of Vittoria, Marquess of Torres Vedras, and Count
of Vimeiro in the peerage of Portugal, Duke of Ciudad Rodrigo
in the peerage of Spain, Knight of the Garter and Grandee of
the First Class, Field-Marshal of the United Kingdom, Marshal
General of Portugal and Captain-General and Marshal of Spain,
waited outside the House of Commons at his own request. 'His
admission being resolved, and a chair being set for him on the
left hand of the bar towards the middle of the House, His Grace
entered, making his obeisances, while all the members rose from
their seats. The Speaker then informing him that a chair was
placed for his repose, he sat down in it for some time covered,
the Serjeant standing on his right hand, with the mace grounded.'
Rising to speak, uncovered, he thanked the House for the latest
of many votes of thanks that they had passed and expressed the
hope that 'it will not be deemed presumptuous in me to take
this opportunity of expressing my admiration of the great efforts
made by this House and the country at a moment of unexampled
pressure and difficulty, in order to support the great scale of
operations by which the contest was brought to so fortunate a
termination.'
Replying, the Speaker referred to 'The military triumphs which

your valor has achieved upon the banks of the Douro and the Tagus, of the Ebro and the Garonne, which have called forth the shouts of admiring nations. These triumphs it is needless to recount. Their names have been written by your conquering sword in the annals of Europe, and we shall hand them down with exultation to our children's children.'[24]

Encouraged by this Sir Hew Dalrymple, three weeks later, wrote to Lord Castlereagh asking for an interview. 'The war in the Peninsula being at an end, Government and the country seem to vie with each other, in testifying their gratitude to those who have contributed by their talents, or their exertions, to the glorious result of the contest; your Lordship, therefore, cannot wonder if I feel myself peculiarly hurt by remaining as I do, under the censure, with which it pleased His Majesty's Ministers to dismiss me from employment in January 1809.'[25] The interview took place soon afterwards and was friendly 'and, in fact, very soon afterwards my name was placed at the head of the list of baronets; and as a mark that the honour was conferred as a reward for public services, it was especially provided, in the patent, that it was given free from all the usual charges.'[26]

There was no such consolation for Sir Harry. On the conclusion of the proceedings of the Board he had resumed his old gentle life as Lieutenant-Colonel of the First Guards. In 1810 he had become Commander of the Brigade of Guards in London. But in his private life he was unfortunate. Already a widower, he lost one son, an aide-de-camp to Moore, at Coruña. Another was a naval officer,* and the third, one of the volunteers from the First Guards, in which he was an ensign, died in the breach at San Sebastian. Sir Harry did not long survive him. He died at Calshott Castle on 18th October 1813.

* He lived until 1870.

References

Chapter 10. 'Considering the Extraordinary Circumstances'

1   SD vi 184. Castlereagh to AW, 4 Nov '08
2   Cintra 11
3   Cintra 181. Evidence of Spencer
4   Croker ii 123
5   Creevey 54. Whitbread to Creevey, 25 Sept '08
6   Creevey 54. Cobbett to Folkestone, 9 Oct '08
7   Cintra 19. Evidence of HD
8   ib
9   Cintra 21–22. Evidence of AW
10 ib 103
11 Cintra 20. Evidence of HD
12 Cintra 104. Evidence of AW
13 SD vi 187. AW to Richmond, 23 Nov '08
14 ib
15 Cintra 206. Evidence of AW
16 Cintra 231–32
17 Cintra 237–38. Opinion of Lord Moira
18 Cintra 556
19 HD 132
20 AR 1809. 225
21 AR 1809. 54
22 Malmesbury ii 85. Ross to Malmesbury, 23 Jan '09
23 SD vi 222. Memorandum by AW, 11 Apr '09
24 WD xii 68
25 HD 136. HD to Castlereagh, 20 July '14
26 ib 137–38

Appendix

Order of Battle of the British Army at dawn 21st August 1808

Commander of the Forces	Lieut.-Gen. Sir Arthur Wellesley
Second in Command	Maj.-Gen. Brent Spencer
Quartermaster-General	Lieut.-Col. James Bathurst
Adjutant-General	Lieut.-Col. John Goulston Tucker
Military Secretary	Lieut.-Col. Henry Torrens
Commander Royal Artillery	Lieut.-Col. William Robe
Commander Royal Engineers	Capt. Howard Elphinstone

Cavalry

20th Light Dragoons (3 sqdns) (Lieut.-Col. Charles Taylor)

Artillery

4th Coy, 5th Bn. R.A. (Capt. Robert Carthew)
3rd Coy, 8th Bn. R.A. (Capt. Richard Raynsford)
9th Coy, 8th Bn. R.A. (Capt. William Morrison)

Infantry

1st Brigade *(Maj.-General Rowland Hill)*

    1st Bn. Fifth (or Northumberland) Regt. (Lieut.-Col. Edward Copson)

    1st Bn. Ninth (or East Norfolk) Regt. (Lieut.-Col. John Cameron)

    1st Bn. Thirty-Eighth (or 1st Staffordshire) Regt. (Lieut-Col. the Hon. Charles Greville)

2nd Brigade *(Maj.-Gen. Ronald Craufurd Ferguson)*

    Thirty-Sixth (or Herefordshire) Regt. (Lieut-Col. Robert Burne)

    1st Bn. Fortieth (or 2nd Somersetshire) Regt. (Lieut.-Col. James Kemmis)

1st Bn. Seventy-First (Highland) Regt. (Lieut.-Col. Dennis Pack)

3rd Brigade *(Brig.-Gen. Miles Nightingall)*
Twenty-Ninth (or Worcestershire) Regt. (Lieut.-Col. Daniel White)
1st Bn. Eighty-Second Regt. (Prince of Wales's Volunteers) (Major Henry Eyre)

4th Brigade *(Brig.-Gen. Barnard Foord Bowes)*
1st Bn. Sixth (or 1st Warwickshire) Regt. (Major Thomas Carnie)
1st Bn. Thirty-Second (or Cornwall) Regt. (Lieut.-Col. Samuel Hinde)

5th Brigade *(Brig.-Gen. Catlin Craufurd)*
1st Bn. Forty-Fifth (or Nottinghamshire) Regt. (Lieut-Col. William Guard)
1st Bn. Ninety-First Regt. (Lieut.-Col. James Robinson)

6th Brigade *(Brig.-Gen. Henry Fane)*
1st Bn. Fiftieth (or West Kent) Regt. (Lieut.-Col. George Walker)
5th Bn. Sixtieth Regt. (Royal Americans) (Major William Davy)
2nd Bn. Ninety-Fifth Regt. (Riflemen) (Major Robert Travers)

7th Brigade *(Brig.-Gen. Robert Anstruther)*
2nd Bn. Ninth (or East Norfolk) Regt. (Lieut.-Col. Henry Craufurd)
2nd Bn. Forty-Third (or Monmouthshire) Regt. (Major Edward Hull)
2nd Bn. Fifty-Second (or Oxfordshire) Regt. (Lieut.-Col. John Ross)
Ninety-Seventh (Queen's Own) Regt. (Lieut.-Col. James Lyon)

8th Brigade *(Brig.-Gen. Wroth Palmer Acland)*
2nd (or Queen's Own) Regt. (Lieut.-Col. William Iremonger)
20th (or East Devonshire) Regt. ($7\frac{1}{2}$ Coys) (Major William Wallace)
1st Bn. Ninety-Fifth Regt. (Riflemen) (2 Coys) (Lieut.-Col. Sidney Beckwith)

Bibliography

with abbreviations used in the references

AR   *The Annual Register* for 1808 and 1809

BRIALMONT AND GLEIG   *History of the Life of Arthur, Duke of Wellington.* M. Brialmont and G. R. Gleig, 1858

CAROLA OMAN   *Sir John Moore.* Carola Oman, 1953

CC   *Correspondence of Viscount Castlereagh.* Ed. Marquess of Londonderry, 1851

CINTRA   *Proceedings upon the Inquiry relative to the Armistice and Convention &c. made and concluded in Portugal in 1808.* 1809

CREEVEY.   *Creevey.* Selected and edited, John Gore, 1948

COLBORNE   *Life of Sir John Colborne, Lord Seton.* Ed. G. C. Moore Smith, 1903

CROKER   *The Croker Papers.* Ed. L. W. Jennings, 1884

DUNCAN   *History of the Royal Artillery.* F. Duncan, 1878

FORTESCUE   *A History of the British Army,* Vol. VI. Sir John Fortescue, 1921

GOMM   *Letters and Journals of Field-Marshal Sir William Gomm.* Ed. F. C. Carr-Gomm, 1881

HARRIS   *Recollections of Rifleman Harris.* Ed. Capt. Curling, 1848

HD   Memoir written by General Sir Hew Dalrymple, Bart. of his proceedings as connected with the affairs of Spain and the commencement of the Peninsular War, 1830

HUSSAR   *The Hussar: the story of Norbert Landsheit, Sergeant in the York Hussars and the 20th Light Dragoons.* Ed. G. R. Gleig, 1837

JOURNAL OF A SOLDIER   *Journal of T.S. of the 71st Highland Light Infantry,* 1828

JOURDAN   *Memoires Militaires du Maréchal Jourdan.* Ed. Vicomte de Grouchy, 1898

LEACH   *Rough Sketches of the Life of an Old Soldier.* Jonathan Leach, 1831

201

LIN *Lettres Inédites de Napoleon 1er.* Ed. Leon Lecestre, 1897

LESLIE *Military Journal of Colonel Leslie of Balquhain,* 1887

MALMESBURY *Letters of the 1st Earl of Malmesbury, his Family and Friends.* Ed. 3rd Earl of Malmesbury, 1870

MC *The Morning Chronicle,* 1808 and 1809

MOORE DIARY *The Diary of Sir John Moore.* Ed. Sir J. F Maurice, 1809

NC *Correspondence de Napoleon 1er.* Vols. XVI–XVIII. 1864

NEALE *Letters from Spain & Portugal:* Adam Neale, M.D., 1809

OMAN *History of the Peninsular War,* Vol. I: Charles Oman, 1802

PS *Peninsular Sketches by Actors on the Scene,* Vol. I. Narrative of Capt Fletcher Wilkie, 45th Regiment. Ed. W. H. Maxwell, 1845

ROSS LEWIN *Life of a Soldier:* H. Ross Lewin, 1834

SCHAUMANN *On the Road with Wellington: the diary of Augustus Ludolf Friedrich Schaumann.* Ed. and trans. Anthony M. Ludovic, 1924

SD *Supplementary Dispatches and Memoranda of Field-Marshal the Duke of Wellington,* Vols. V, VI and XIII. Ed. 2nd Duke of Wellington, 1858–72

SHERER *Recollections of the Peninsula.* G. Moyle Sherer (2nd Edn), 1825

SIMMONS *A British Rifleman. The Journals and Correspondence of Major George Simmons.* Ed. W. Verner, 1899

STANHOPE *Notes of Conversations with the Duke of Wellington.* The Earl of Stanhope, 1889

THIEBAULT *Memoirs of Baron Thiebault.* Tr. A. J. Butler, 1896

VERNER *History and Campaigns of the Rifle Brigade:* Vol. I. Willoughby Verner, 1812

WD *The Dispatches of Field-Marshal the Duke of Wellington,* Vols. IV and XII. Ed. J. Gurwood, 1834–39

WARRE *Letters from the Peninsula, 1808–12.* Sir William Warre (Ed. E. Warre), 1909

WATSON *The Reign of George III.* J. Seton Watson, 1960

WYLDMEM *Memoir annexed to Wyld's Atlas showing the principal Movements, Battles and Sieges in which the British Troops bore a Conspicuous Part*

INDEX

Lake, General Gerard, 1st Viscount. 82.
La Lippe, Fort. 143.
Landsheit, Serj Norbert. 102–3.
Lavos. 74.
Lefebvre, François Joseph, Marshal, Duke of Danzig. 52.
Leiria. 77, 78, 93, 98, 137.
Ligonier, Field-Marshal Jean Louis, 1st Earl. 10.
Lisbon. 17, 18, 40, 41, 54, 55, 62, 70, 71, 72, 73, 77, 80, 84, 87, 90, 91, 93, 94, 95, 96, 97, 98, 106, 107, 122, 123, 127, 131, 132, 135, 137, 144, 146, 147, 148, 149, 150, 151, 154, 159, 163, 169, 175, 186, 195.
Loison, General Louis Henri. 77, 80, 81, 84, 108, 111, 159, 163.
Lourinha. 91, 92, 93, 102, 104, 111, 112, 119, 120, 121.
Lugar. 76.

Maçeira Bay. 84, 91, 92, 93, 98, 103, 108, 129, 144, 146, 147.
Maçeira river. 93, 102, 103.
Madeira. 38.
Madrid. 19, 20, 22, 23, 52, 54, 126, 153, 176.
Mafra. 95, 96, 130, 131, 132, 151, 159, 161.
Maida, Battle of. 15, 106.
Malcolm, Capt. Pulteney, R.N. 89, 90, 144, 185.
Maria-Luisa, Queen of Spain. 18, 19.
Mariano hill and ridge. 104, 108, 114, 119, 120(fn).
Marlborough, John Churchill, 1st Duke of. 9.
Masséna, André, Marshal Prince of Essling. 138.
Materosa, Viscount. 26, 28, 30.
Medina de Rio Seco, Battle of. 53, 54.
Melbourne, William Lamb, 2nd Viscount. 194.
Mellish, Capt. Henry Francis. 123.
Minden. 10, 110.
M'Kayes, Piper. 121.

Moira, General Francis Rawdon Hastings, 2nd Earl of. 178, 192.
Mondego Bay. 56, 75, 84, 88, 90, 93, 97, 98, 99, 126, 128, 159, 189.
Mondego river. 56, 57, 73, 88.
Montechique. 83, 84, 91, 132.
Montemor-o-Velho. 75.
Monte Junta. 84, 121.
Moore, Lieut.-Gen. Sir John. 10, 20, 21, 36, 38, 39, 47, 59, 60, 63, 64, 65, 66, 67, 68, 83, 86, 88, 90, 91, 92, 96, 97, 98, 99, 105, 131–34, 143, 146, 147, 148, 149, 150, 155, 156, 171, 177, 185, 189, 191, 194, 195, 196, 197.
Mornington, Garrett Wesley, 1st Earl of. 35.
Mulgrave, Henry Phipps, 3rd Baron. 30.
Murat, Joachim, Marshal Grand Duke of Berg (later King of Naples). 19, 20.
Murray, Capt. & Lieut.-Col. George. 95, 122, 129, 144, 145, 146, 147, 150.

Napoleon I. 15, 16, 17, 18, 19, 20, 22, 40, 42, 46, 70, 72, 106, 107, 110(fn), 137, 139, 165, 175, 176.
Neale, Adam, Surgeon. 94.
Nelson, Vice-Admiral Horatio, 1st Viscount. 31.
Nicholls, Lieut.-Gen. Oliver. 178, 192.
Nightingall, Brig.-Gen. Miles. 105, 120.
Nugent, Lieut.-Gen. Sir George. 178.

Obidos. 79, 88, 92.
Oporto. 18, 40, 44, 55, 57, 62, 72, 78, 86, 87, 88, 130, 145, 148, 162, 165, 167, 170.
Ordnance Board of. 37, 46, 94.
Oswald, Capt., R.N. 128.

Paget, Lieut.-Gen. Henry, Lord (later Marquess of Anglesey). 60, 68, 150, 195.

206